Stress Free Quilting™
Quick and Easy Hexagon Quilts

Quilter on the Run Press

Quilter on the Run
quilterontherun.com
© K. Vierra
Kris@quilterontherun.com

D1294330

Stress Free Quilting™
Quick and Easy Hexagon Quilts

©2020 by Kris Vierra

Editor: Sandra K Petersen

Library of Congress Control Number: 2021902508
Vierra, Kristin Jeane
        Stress Free Quilting™ Quick and Easy Hexagon Quilts/
Kristin Vierra.
ISBN 978-1-7322162-4-2

Quilter on the Run Press

3807 NW 63rd Terrace
Kansas City, MO 64151
402-613-8545
www.quilterontherun.com

Disclaimer

✳ Contents ✳

About Stress Free Quilting.. 1

Introduction... 2

Author's Note.. 5

How to use this Book.. 6

Setting up Your Workspace.. 7

Hexagon Sizing Chart... 9

Notes on Fabric... 10

Helpful Tools... 11

The Hexies.. 12

Prepping the Hexies... 13

Sewing the Hexies.. 17

The Quilts

Flower Power... 19

Quilter's Garden.. 25

Tulips on Parade.. 31

Under the Sea.. 39

Up, Up, and Away.. 51

Flutterby Butterfly.. 61

Bargello De Hexies... 71

Diamonds are a Girl's Best Friend 85

Star Brite 99

Hexagon Jubilee 115

Yoga Poses 133

Just Breathe 141

Resources 149

About the Author 150

Acknowledgments 151

The best way to get started Is to quit talking and begin doing." – Walt Disney

About *Stress Free Quilting*™

After working, and teaching, in the quilting industry for over a decade, I am still constantly surprised at the number of people who are worried and stressed out about how their projects will turn out. They are convinced the "Quilt Police" exist, and there is only one "right" way to do a project. Quilting is supposed to be fun and stress free. I created this series to encourage people to explore old and new quilting techniques without all the stress and worry. Keep in mind that stress free does not necessarily mean easy. Hopefully, you will find this to be a relaxing, less complicated way to approach quilting that helps you to reset, recharge, and reboot after the hustle and bustle of everyday life.

Each *Stress Free Quilting*™ book is designed to not only help you learn and expand your quilting skills, but also to learn how to de-stress, increase your motivation, and to remember to take time out for yourself. In each section, in addition to the quilting lesson, you will find suggestions for Yoga poses to relieve tension and stress and tips to aid with time management and self care.

Star Brite Page 99

Introduction

My mom taught me the sewing basics when I was a young girl, and I continued on through 4-H learning how to make and sew garments. It wasn't until my sister had her first baby, 24 years ago, that I even thought about making a quilt. I started off with that first simple baby quilt and became enthralled with the fascinating and incredibly complex patterns that could be made just by combining fabrics and geometric designs. I became especially intrigued with hexagon quilts. At that time, the only way I knew how to quilt anything, other than a baby quilt, was by hand, and I will freely admit that I am not a good hand quilter. I knew your stitches were supposed to be nice and even, but mine were always more like Morse code. You know dot, dot, dash, dash, dash. If I'm being honest, I'm not really good at any kind of hand-work. I just don't have the patience, or time, it takes to become truly proficient. Because of this, I tended to limit myself to small simple square or strip quilt projects, quilts that lend themselves to being tied, but I still dreamed about all of those incredible designs.

Fast forward 12 years to when I acquired my longarm machine. This opened up all kinds of quilting possibilities for me. I will concede that my piecing skills were nowhere near as refined as my quilting skills. Starting out as a seamstress, it took me a while to realize that ¼" seams were more than a suggestion. The concepts of sharp points, long straight seams, and smooth curves were great, but how did I achieve them? In addition, there were all these "rules" that I thought I had to follow. Like Y-seams were the only way to connect certain blocks, or the only way to make a hexagon quilt was by hand.

Feeling overwhelmed by these "rules," yet still liking the more complex designs, I started designing my own quilts. These were either: A. whole cloths that didn't require me to piece anything, or B. pictorial quilts that allowed me to do anything I wanted. They didn't have to follow any set "rules," as you could always say that something was "an artistic element" and people wouldn't question it, but I never forgot those gorgeous, intricately pieced quilts that I first saw when I started with that initial baby quilt. In fact, I had a picture of an antique quilt that I had seen in a book back in 2009, which I could not get out of my head. It was made up of 130, 2" Lemoyne stars that seemed to float across the top of the quilt.

The problem was figuring out how to reproduce it. The diamonds needed to make those blocks were only 1¹⁄₁₆ of an inch with the seam allowance! I tried piecing them by machine without any luck. It's really hard to sew a ½" Y-Seam. Next, I tried having a custom die made to cut them all exactly the same, which helped, but it wasn't enough. I even tried piecing them by hand I was that desperate. Over the course of the next seven years, I would bring out the fabric and try something different. I just couldn't get this quilt out of my head. Finally, it dawned on me. I was still trying to follow the traditional "rules." Why? Had I not learned anything over the last nine years? Who said there was only one way to make a particular block?

I started thinking about some of the techniques I had used to design my art quilts, and how I might apply these techniques to this star block. It took a few tries, but I finally figured it out. (See the picture below of the finished block. Note the thimble for reference. FYI, the name of the quilt is Insanity.)

Then I got to thinking, I could adapt this same technique to other blocks as well. All those hexagon quilts that I had been so fascinated by were now within my reach! And the best part, not only was the method quick and easy; it was accurate too.

This book will take you through all the steps you will need to learn how to start making your own gorgeous hexagon quilts. The quilts are in order by difficulty level. Even if you are an accomplished quilter, I recommend starting off with one of the easier projects until you have mastered the technique. If you are just starting out, don't worry. If you follow the how-to section step-by step, you'll be making perfect hexagon quilts in no time. After that, the sky's the limit!

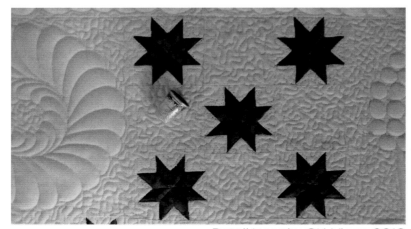

Detail Insanity ©K. Vierra 2016

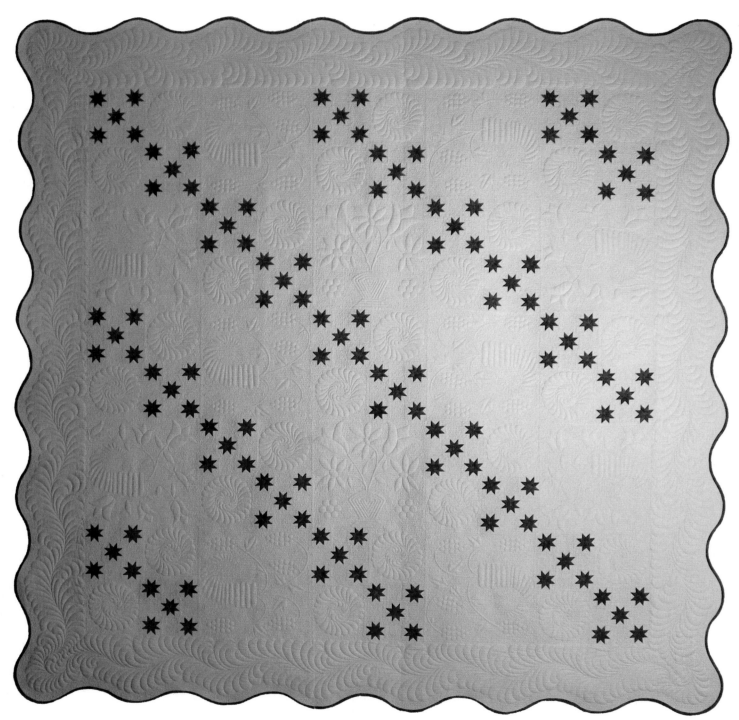

Insanity Finished Quilt Size 82" X 82" Pieced and quilted by the author. ©K. Vierra 2016

Author's Note

I absolutely hate the words "quilt as desired." I think this phrase should be considered a four letter word. There is nothing worse than getting to the end of a detailed project, pages and pages of instructions on how to construct a top, only to read those dreaded three words "Quilt as Desired."

When I first started quilting, I never knew what I desired. Frequently, my finished tops sat for months, or even years, while I tried to figure out what to quilt on them. I vowed, if I ever started writing books or selling patterns, that I would not do this to another person. You will find detailed explanations on how you can quilt each project in this book. Please feel free to use them exactly, or as a jumping off point to inspire your own creative ideas. Remember there are no rules. Just enjoy yourself and have fun.

Double Irish Chain block from *Stress Free Quilting*™ Quilt as Desired; So I got it Pieced, Now What?

How To Use This Book

This book is designed with the projects getting progressively more difficult as you proceed. While you certainly can start with any project, I recommend that you start with Flower Power. Even if you only do this one project before moving on to one of the bed sized quilts, I think you will find you will have less frustration with the method. Starting with a small quilt will help you to master the technique before having to manipulate large sections of fabric.

All of the smaller wall hangings, with the exception of Bargello De Hexagons are made using ⅝" hexies. Bargello and the bed sized quilts are all made with 1" hexies. Hexagons are sized by side length. (See the diagram page 9 for hexagon sizing information.)

Please make sure that you read all of the prepping the hexies instructions, on page 13, before starting any project. With this method in particular, precision is very important. The more precisely you prepare your hexagons, the better your results. That being said, you can still maneuver the hexies fairly easily, if you need to get a better fit.

I highly recommend when learning any new piecing technique practicing on scrap material. In this case, I would start by making one of the Standard Flower sections to familiarize yourself with the process (instructions on page 18). Make sure your machine is setup properly, before actually using your project fabric.

Quilters love to share, and I'm no exception. I would love to see any and all projects made from this book. Please feel free to share on my Facebook page (www.facebook.com/quilterontherun), or send me an email (kris@ quilterontherun.com). Happy Piecing!

Setting Up Your Workspace

Before you start working on any quilting projects, create a defined space specifically for you and your projects. Whereas you can work at the kitchen table, it is important for you to have your own space. This is your place to go to escape from daily stressors and to have time that is just for you. You deserve to have a little me time and space. Without this defined space, it becomes much harder to carve out time to work on your projects. If you know that you must haul everything out and then get it all put away again, in a short period of time, it makes it harder to start at all.

Once you have found a dedicated space to use, you need to set it up so that it works for you. The size of your workspace is not nearly as important as how you have it set up. You can have a gigantic space to work in, but if you can't find anything, you're never going to be productive. I firmly believe that if you can't find something, you don't actually have it. You can find inexpensive modular shelving and organizers at most big box stores such as: Walmart, IKEA, JoAnn's, or Michael's. Most of these offer 50% off sales throughout the year to help keep your costs down. Trying grouping like items together to help save space. (For example, have one drawer for all your cutting supplies, i.e. scissors, rotary cutters, snips, instead of a drawer for each.) Make sure that you label your drawers so that you can easily find the one you are looking for when you need something.

After you have organized all your sewing supplies, you want to think about how you want to set up your actual workspace. I like to have my ironing board close to my sewing machine so that I am not constantly having to get up and down. If you don't have the space for a full-sized ironing board next to your machine, try using a covered pad that you can set on a small table next to you. You can find these at most sewing shops (See Fig. 1), or you can easily make one with some plywood, batting, and duck cloth. I like to set mine up similar to the triangle set up recommended for kitchens, but instead of stove, sink, fridge, substitute sewing machine, ironing board, cutting surface. This keeps everything in a convenient space that doesn't require unnecessary extra work. (See Fig 2)

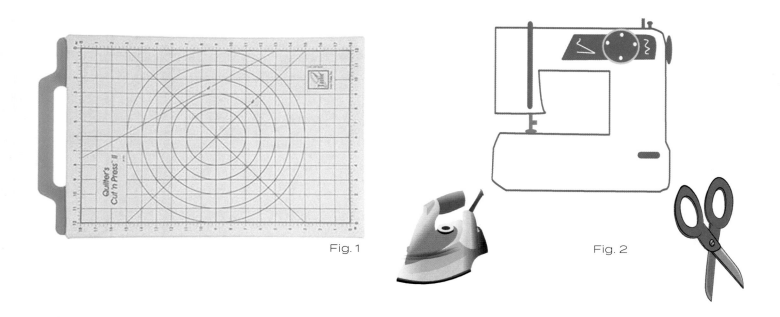

Fig. 1

Fig. 2

However you decide to set up your space, the most important thing to remember is that it is yours. This is your place to go to relax and take time to recharge doing something you enjoy.

The worst thing one can do is not to try, to be aware of what one wants and not give in to it, to spend years in silent hurt wondering if something could have materialized - never knowing.
Jim Rohn

Hexagon Sizing Information

Hexagon Size	Cut Strip Width	# of Pieces a Strip Yields	# of Pieces per Fat Quarter	# of Pieces per 1/4 Yard	# of Pieces per 1/2 yard	# of Pieces per 1 Yard
5/8"	1 3/4"	26	96	96	192	384
3/4"	2"	20	90	90	180	360
1"	2 1/2"	16	57	57	114	228
1 1/4"	3"	13	40	40	80	160
1 1/2"	3 1/2"	11	29	29	58	116

Notes on Fabric

I personally recommend pre-washing all of your fabrics. It is very easy to add back in a little extra body or stiffness to the fabric using a spray starch or Best Press ™. It does take a little extra time, but is preferable to having your beautiful quilt marred by a fabric that bled.

This method does not require you to be concerned with whether you are cutting on the straight or cross grain.

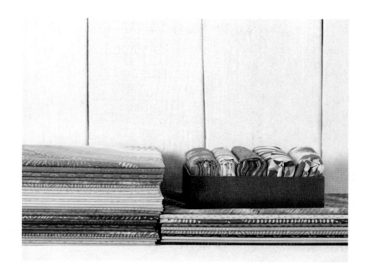

Position of the hexies is largely based on personal preference, and efficient use of fabric. Depending on the pattern, you may want to fussy cut your hexagons to achieve a particular pattern, or highlight a section of the fabric. For instance, positioning the fabric in the center hexagon of each flower to focus on something special. (See Fig. 1)

Fig 1

While fabric grain doesn't matter, fabric weave does. Fabrics that fray easily, are very thin, or have an open weave, will make handling and working with the hexagons more difficult.

Helpful Tools

Foundation Paper- this special paper turns to a soft dissolving fiber when it becomes wet, eliminating the need to remove it. It is thicker than standard wash-away paper allowing you to be able to turn edges with ease. You can order it from www.quilterontherun.com

Mono-
Poly Thread- Superior®, Madeira® or Sulky® work best

Machine top-stitch needles-75/11

Elmer's™ Washable School Glue Sticks- use only this type of glue sticks; don't use the disappearing purple sticks. (Elmer's™ will not harm your quilts, as it is just starch and water.)

Manicure cuticle sticks

Hard Pressing Surface

Freezer paper

Fabric and Paper Scissors

Sewing machine-with an adjustable zigzag stitch

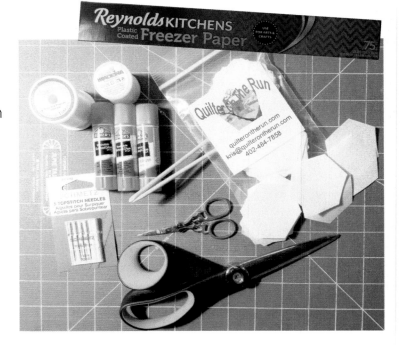

Tools for cutting out Hexies-scissors, Accu-cutter™, Brother Scan and Cut™, rotary cutter, and hexie templates or rulers.

The Hexies

Precision is very important to the success of this method, and starts with the foundation hexagons. There are many different ways to make your hexagon templates. The easiest is to buy them pre-cut by a laser. This ensures that every hexagon will be exactly the same. You can also cut your own, if you have access to a cutting machine. Brother Scan and Cut™, Cricut™, Accu-cut™ or any equivalent works well. Or, my least favorite method, hexagons can be traced on the stabilizer using a hexagon template, and cut out by hand.

 Note: Accu-Cut dies already include seam allowances. If you use one to cut your stabilizer, your hexagons will be ½" bigger than the size marked on the die.

Prepping the Hexies

Pre-wash and dry your fabric. After washing, press fabric with a steam iron. This would be the time to add starch. Note: This is the only time you will use steam. When working with the hexies make sure that you use a DRY IRON ONLY! The stabilizer used in this method is water soluble. It will start to dissolve if you use too much steam.

Apply a thin layer of glue to one precut hexagon foundation and affix it to the WRONG SIDE of your fabric. Be sure to leave ¼" seam allowance on all sides of each of the hexagon. Continue applying hexagons in this manner (See Fig. 1)

Fig. 1

Tip: Iron your freezer paper to your ironing board for an instant workspace. When it gets too much glue on it, just iron another piece on top and continue working.

Tip: I like to cut strips of fabric wide enough to accommodate 3-4 hexagons across. These smaller sections are easier to manipulate when gluing and ironing.

Heat set hexagons with a DRY
IRON after gluing. This helps the
glue to dry quickly, and holds your
hexagons more firmly in place.
Press only, do not move the iron
back and forth over the paper.

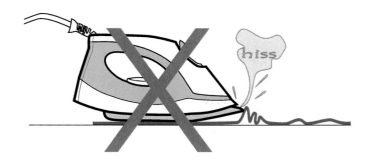

 Tip: Place hexagons on
point for the most efficient
use of fabric. (See Fig. 2)

Cut around stabilizer leaving
approximately ¼" seam allowance.
This does not need to be exact. If
you want them all to be perfect,
you can use your rotary cutter and
cut each of them out. However,
this takes considerably more time.
Personally think it is more fun to
sew than to cut. (See Fig. 3)

Fig. 2

Fig. 3

 Note: Exception to rough ¼", if
you are facing your quilt, you
will need to make sure that
you have an exact 1/4" seam
allowance.

Apply a thin layer of Elmer's School Glue™ to two opposing sides of the hexagon. Fold seam allowance towards stabilizer. If you are having difficulty turning the edges, try using the flat side of the manicure stick. Repeat on opposite sides until all sides of the hexagon have been turned towards the stabilizer. (Figs. 1-3)

Fig. 1

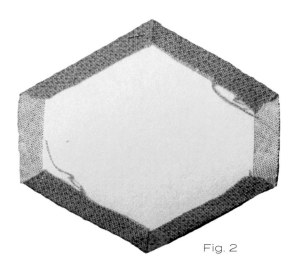

Fig. 2

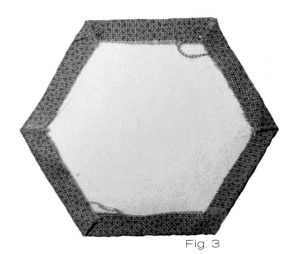

Fig. 3

I recommend using a hexagon template on all of your hexagons in the beginning, to check for accuracy. The more hexagons you make, the better, and faster, you will get at folding the fabric on to the foundation paper. As you become more proficient, you may only need to spot check one out of every 10-15 hexagons. (See Fig. 4)

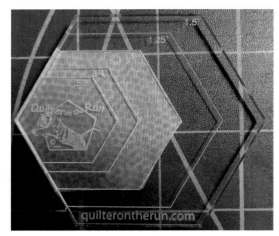

Fig. 4

Be gentle when turning hexie sides. The more precisely you turn the fabric onto the foundation hexagon, the better the final fit of the top. Watch out for overturning the sides. This results when you have too much glue which softens the paper, or just being a little to rough. When this happens, both the fabric and the foundation paper get turned under, creating a dip in the side. (See Fig. 5)

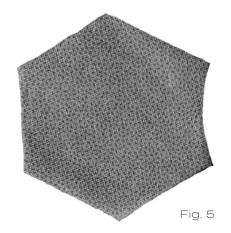

Fig. 5

The reverse occurs when you don't turn the fabric over onto the foundation paper far enough. This causes the hexagons to have an irregular shape, and will affect how well the hexagons fit together in the finished top. (See Fig. 6)
Both under turning and over turning will cause problems during the assembly process. You might not notice it as much when joining together individual hexies, but as you continue to assemble the quilt, it will become more pronounced. Just like in standard piecing when you don't have an accurate ¼" seam allowance.

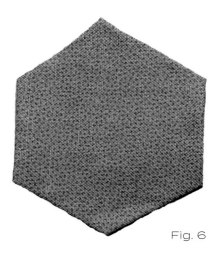

Fig. 6

Tip: If using a template with seam allowances shown, use the finished hexagon size for spot checking.

Sewing The Hexies

Set your sewing machine to a zig-zag stitch. I recommend a very short stitch length, and a narrow width. When you are just starting out, you may want to increase your stitch width, but don't change your stitch length. You will also need to decrease your top tension on your sewing machine when you are using mono-poly thread. (The settings shown in Fig. 1 are for my Bernina. You will need to adjust accordingly for your machine.)

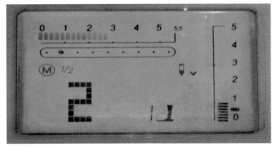

Fig. 1

Take two hexies and butt the edges closely together. Make sure that they are closely touching, but not overlapping. Align the top and bottom edges making sure that they are even. (See Fig 2)

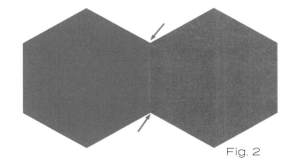

Fig. 2

Secure your starting stitch and continue stitching using your narrow zig-zag stitch. Make sure that the needle goes from one hexie to the other. This will ensure that your hexies are securely fastened to each other. (See Fig 3)

Fig. 3

Each quilt pattern shows the most efficient hexagon groupings. Following the pattern order, sew your next hexagon in place. (See Fig. 4 page 18)

Tip: Be careful placing light hexagons on a dark background. The stabilizer keeps the dark fabric from initially shadowing through, but it will be washed away.

The central unit of most hexagon quilts is the standard flower section. Sew hexagons in the order shown in Fig. 5. The most efficient way to quilt a standard flower section is to stitch down one side, backtrack, and then stitch up the opposite side. (See stitching diagram.) This eliminates the need to constantly stop and start. Continue in this fashion until entire flower section is assembled.

Fig. 4

Sew the required number of each hexagon grouping together, as per the pattern directions. After all groupings have been completed, join sections together as directed in the pattern. If needed, you can ease sections together. Don't worry if sections bow slightly. They will flatten out when washed.

For quilts that have the hexagons set on top of a background fabric, apply a thin layer of glue to the entire hexagon figure and center onto the background fabric. Use the placement diagram as a reference. Heat set and then sew along the edge, use the same zig-zag stitch used to assemble the hexies. Make sure that the needle catches the hexie with one stitch and the background fabric with the next stitch.

Fig 5

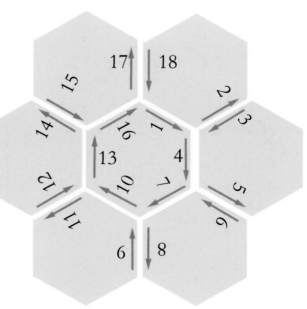

Stitching Diagram

Flower Power

Finished Quilt Size 25" X 31"

Get your groove on with this sixties inspired flower power wall hanging that's just the right size to brighten any room.

Hexie Requirements

6 yellow hexagons

6 blue hexagons

52 green hexagons

30 red hexagons

13 purple hexagons

18 orange hexagons

Total number of hexagon foundations needed for this project: 125.

Materials

Yardage is based on 42" wide fabric

1 yd med purple tonal (includes fabric for borders and binding)

¼ yd medium green print

⅛ yd bright yellow print

⅛ yd bright orange print

¼ yd bright red tonal

⅛ yd bright blue print

1 yd light blue

1 yard of your choice of coordinating fabric for backing.

 War is not healthy for children and other living things. Lorraine Schneider.

Assembling the Quilt

Prepare the required number of each color hexagons, as per the instructions in the Prepping The Hexies section. (Page 13)

From light blue fabric cut:

(1) 25½" X 31½"

From med/dark purple tonal cut:

(2) 1½" X 29½"

(2) 1½" X 25½"

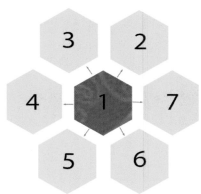

Fig. 1

1. Sew together (1) yellow and (1) purple hexagon. Continue around the center hexagons to create the center standard flower, as per instructions in Sewing the Hexagons on page 18. (See Fig. 1)

2. Sew the next row onto the flower alternating red and blue hexagons. Make sure that the blue hexagons are sewn into the "V's" and the red hexagons are sewn on to the flat sides of the yellow hexagons. (See Fig. 2)

Fig. 2

3. Sew a third row of red hexagons on to this unit. (See Fig. 3)

4. Sew together two orange hexagons to make a double orange unit.

5. Next make a double unit using one purple and one red hexagon; repeat for a total of (6) double orange and (6) double red/purple units.

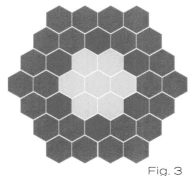

Fig. 3

6. Sew a third orange hexagon on to the (2) orange hexagon unit; repeat for a total of (6) units. (See Fig. 4)

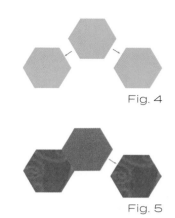

Fig. 4

7. Sew an additional purple hexagon on to the red and purple hexagon unit; repeat for a total of (6) units. (See Fig. 5)

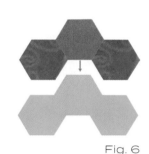

Fig. 5

8. Connect (1) orange hexagon unit to (1) red and purple unit. (See Fig. 6)

9. Attach orange, red, and purple units to center flower section. (See Fig. 7)

10. Sew together (2) green hexagons; repeat for a total of four units. Sew together (3) green hexagons; repeat until you have (7) units. Sew together (4) green hexagons. Sew these units together to form leaves (See Fig. 8 and Fig. 9)

Fig. 6

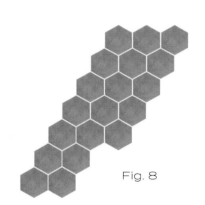

Fig. 8

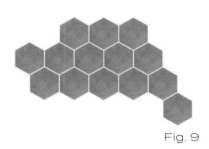

Fig. 9

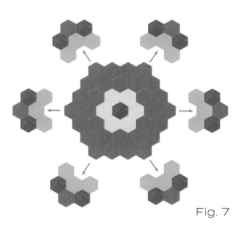

Fig. 7

11. Using placement diagram on page 23, sew together remaining green hexagons to form flower stem. Join flower and leaves to stem.

12. Apply a thin layer of glue to wrong side of finished flower and center on blue background fabric using placement diagram on page 23 as a guide.

13. Apply purple borders to sides and top. Press seams away from center. Quilt as per quilting diagram on page 24. Background was quilted using a meandering filigree type design. Leaves were outlined and details were added to form spines. Swirls were quilted onto the flower petals

Placement Diagram

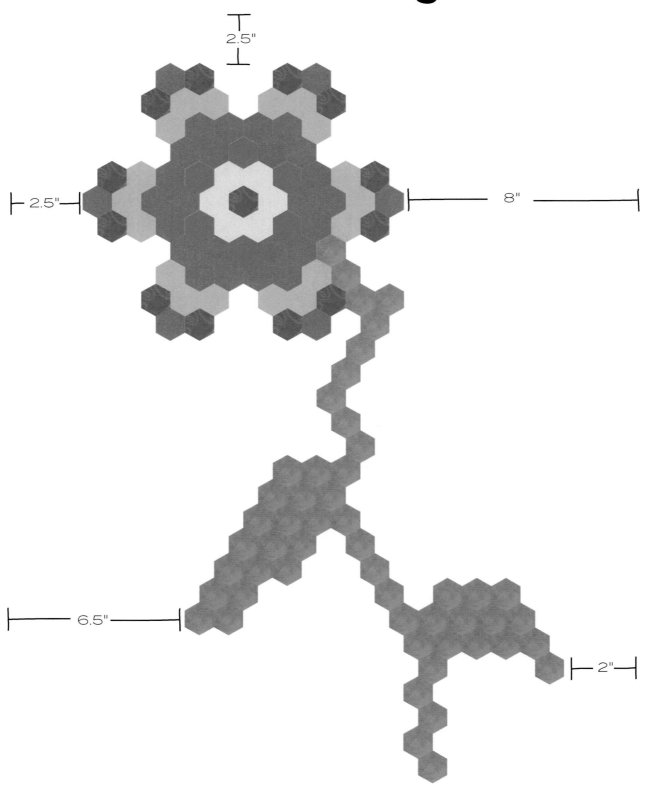

Quilting Diagram

A Quilter's Garden

Finish Quilt Size 48" X 66"

Lap quilts provide a cozy feeling no matter what the weather. Snuggle up under this cute hexie quilt with twinkling star flowers climbing this easy vine.

Hexie Requirements

 140 green hexagons

 94 purple hexagons

 94 blue hexagons

 94 red hexagons

 21 yellow hexagons

Total number of hexagon foundations needed for this project: 443

Materials

Yardage is based on 42" wide fabric

 2 yds med/dark purple print (includes border and binding)

 1¾ yds medium blue print (includes inner border)

 1⅝ yd light blue fabric

 ¼ yd med/dark red print

 ⅛ yd medium yellow print

 ⅜ yd medium green tonal

3 yds of your choice of coordinating fabric for backing. (Backing will be seamed.)

 Flowers don't worry about how they're going to bloom. They just open up and turn toward the light, and that makes them beautiful.
Jim Carrey

Assembling the Quilt

Prepare the required number of each color hexagons, as per the instructions in the Prepping the Hexies section. (Page 13)

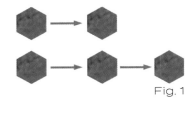

Fig. 1

From blue fabric cut:

(2) 2½" X 54½"

(2) 2½ X 40½"

From purple fabric cut:

(2) 4½" X 58½"

(2) 4½" X 48½"

From light blue background cut:

(1) 36½ X 54½"

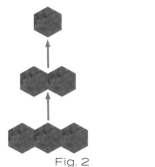

Fig. 2

1. Join together (2) blue hexagons; repeat until you have (12) units. Add a third blue hexagon to half of the units. Repeat for each of the red and purple hexagon flowers. (See Fig. 1)

2. Using (1) additional blue hexagon, join your (3) hexagon unit to a your (2) hexagon unit, placing one additional hexagon on top, as per Fig. 2. For each color flower: red, blue and purple, make (6) units.

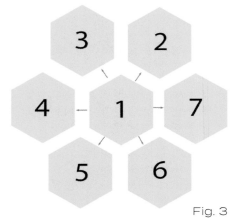

Fig. 3

3. Begin by sewing together (2) yellow hexagons. Referring to Fig. 3, continue to add hexagons in numerical order until center yellow unit is completed.

4. Continue, referring to Fig. 4, to sew three concentric rows of blue hexagons around this yellow center. Repeat process to make red and purple flower centers.

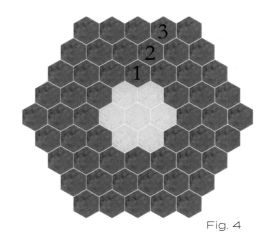

Fig. 4

5. Attach units made in steps 1 and 2 to the flower center made in step 4. (See Fig. 5)

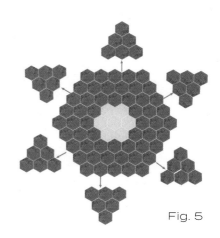

Fig. 5

6. Using placement diagram on page 29 as a reference, join together green hexagons to form vines. I find it's easiest to string piece a bunch of hexies into units of two, and then start to join those double units together to make larger units. Do not join all of the hexagons into double units, as you will need some odd numbered ones. Continue joining green hexagons until vine is completed. Attach vine to flowers.

7. Apply a thin layer of glue to the back of the finished unit. Using placement guide on page 29 as a reference, affix hexagons to the 36½" X 54½" piece of light blue back ground fabric. Heat fix with dry iron, and sew together using zig-zag stitch.

8. Apply borders to sides of quilt using a ¼" seam allowance. Press all seams away from center. Repeat with inner top/bottom blue border strips, adjusting as needed to fit quilt. Using same ¼" seam allowance apply to top and bottom of quilt. Allow extra length, if mitering the corners.

9. Repeat using outer purple side, and top/bottom, borders.

10. Refer to quilting diagram on page 30 for quilting ideas. Quilt was quilted using freehand feathers around the outer border, and loops in the inner border. A simple swirl sets off the flower vines, and is echoed inside the main hexagon flowers. A generic meander was used to quilt the background. Optional-I recommend outline quilting around the outer edge of the hexagons for more definition.

If you find your neck gets sore while cutting out and prepping hexies- try Corpse/Savasana Pose or Extended Puppy Pose/Uttana Shishosana Page 133 & 134.

Placement Diagram

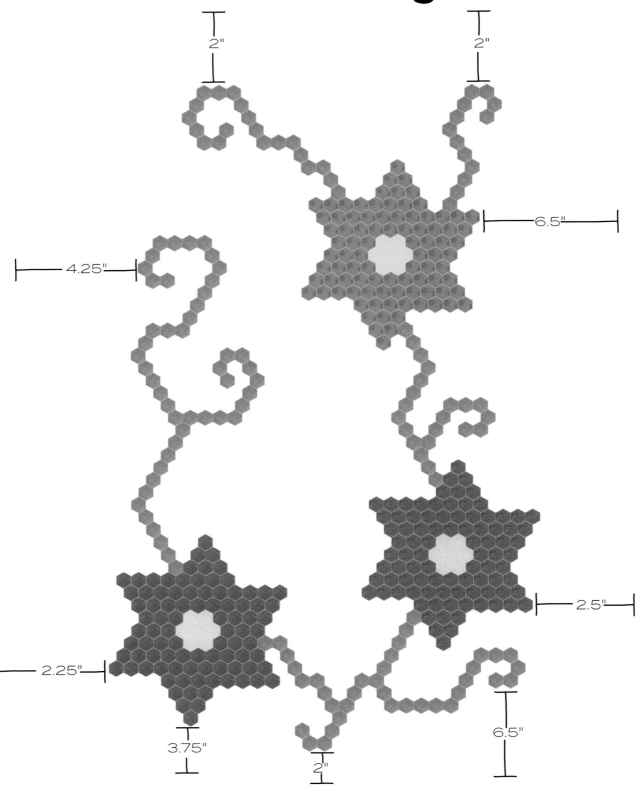

Quilting Diagram

Tulips on Parade

Finished Quilt Size 45"X65"

 Flowers always make people better, happier, and more helpful; they are sunshine, food, and medicine for the soul.
Luther Burbank

You don't have to wait for spring to enjoy the tulips. This jubilee of hexie flowers will let you plant a truly colorful garden any time of year.

Hexie Requirements

 12 medium pink hexagons

 43 red hexagons

 43 purple hexagons

 12 light purple hexagons

 43 med. orange hexagons

 12 dark orange hexagons

 80 lt./med. green hexagons

162 med/dark green hexagons

Total number of hexagon foundations needed for this project: 407.

Materials

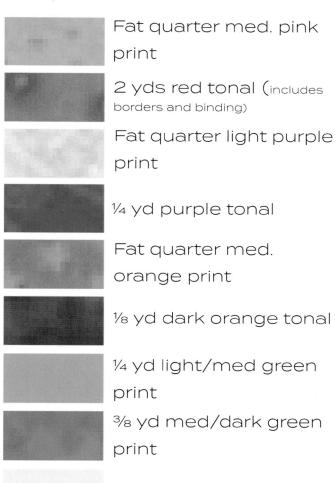

Yardage is based on 42" wide fabric

Fat quarter med. pink print

2 yds red tonal (includes borders and binding)

Fat quarter light purple print

¼ yd purple tonal

Fat quarter med. orange print

⅛ yd dark orange tonal

¼ yd light/med green print

⅜ yd med/dark green print

1⅓ yds light blue fabric

1½ yds of your choice of coordinating fabric for backing.

Assembling the Quilt

Prepare the required number of each color hexagons, as per the instructions in the Prepping the Hexies section. (Page 13)

From light blue fabric cut:

(1) 31½" X 44½"

From purple tonal cut

(2) 2½" X 31½"

(2) 2½" X 48½"

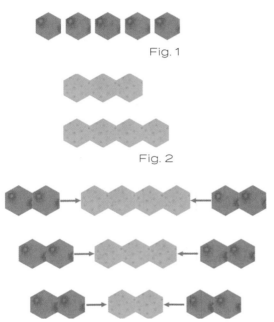

Fig. 1

Fig. 2

Fig. 3

1. Join together (5) red hexagons; repeat with purple and orange hexagons. (See Fig. 1)

2. Join (2) red hexies, repeat for a total of (16) double hexie units; repeat process with purple and orange hexagons.

3. Join together (2) pink; repeat until you have (4) double pink units. Repeat this process using the light purple and dark orange hexagons.

4. Using (3) of the pink double hexie units made in Step 2, add one additional pink hexagon to one of the double units to make a (3) hexie chain, and join the other (2) of them together to make a chain of (4) hexagons; repeat with the light purple and dark orange units. (See Fig. 2)

5. Join one double red hexagon unit to either side of the (2), (3) and (4) pink chains previously made; repeat with the light purple and dark orange units, using the previously made purple and orange units respectively. (See Fig. 3)

6. Join a pink hexagon to a red hexagon, repeat for a total of (2) units. Repeat process using light purple and dark orange hexagons

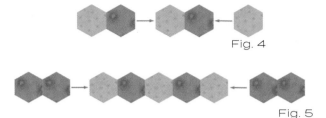

Fig. 4

7. Join the pink/red unit to the other pink/red unit and add one additional pink unit to the end. This will make a (5) hexagon chain. Repeat using light purple/purple, dark orange/orange units. (See Fig. 4)

Fig. 5

8. Using the double hexagon units from step 2, join one double red unit to each side of the (5) hexagon chain made in the previous step. Repeat using purple and orange units. (See Fig. 5)

9. Using the red double hexagons units from step 2, join (4) double hexagons together to make one chain (8) hexagons long.

10. Join (3) additional red double hexies together to make a chain (6) hexies long. Add one red hexagon to the end of this chain for a total of (7) hexies; repeat using purple and orange units.

11. Using the red double hexie units from step 2, add a single hexagon to the top of one of the double red units to form a pyramid shape; repeat for a total of (3) units. Repeat this using the purple and orange double units. (See Fig. 6)

12. Add an additional red hexie to (1) of the remaining red double hexagon units to form a (3) hexie chain.

13. Join one of the pyramids to the (3) hexagon chain made in step 12 Repeat using purple and orange hexagons. (See Fig. 7)

Fig. 6

14. Using Fig. 8 (page 35) as a guide sew the previously made rows together to create the tulips.

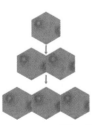

Fig. 7

15. Join together (2) dark green hexagons; repeat for a total of (22) double hexie units. Add one dark green hexagon to the top of one of these double units; repeat for a total of (20) units. (See Fig. 9)

16. Join (10) of the units made in the previous step together to form the stem. Add the remaining double dark green hexagon unit to the bottom of this chain; repeat to form both dark green stems. (See Fig 10)

17. Using the same technique create and join together (6) light green units. (See Fig. 11)

18. Using Figures 12-17 on page 36 as a reference, join together remaining dark and light green hexagons to form the leaves. Figures go in order from left to right for leaf placement.

19. Join leaves to each side of previously made stems and sew tulip to tops of stems using placement guide on page 37 as a reference.

20. Connect the (3) tulips to each other. Apply a thin layer of glue to the back of the tulips and center them on the light blue fabric. Heat set with a dry iron, and zigzag around the outside edge to secure them to the background fabric. (If you are having trouble maneuvering the larger unit, you can glue each tulip on individually. Just remember to zigzag the units together once they are on the background fabric. This avoids having any loose edges.)

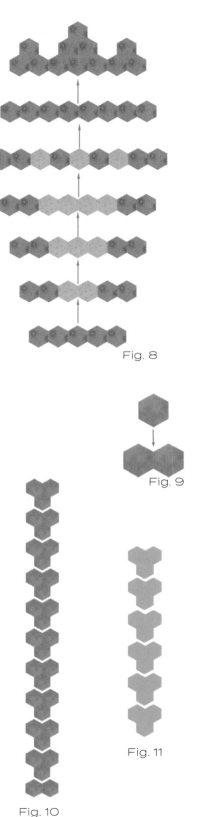

Fig. 8

Fig. 9

Fig. 11

Fig. 10

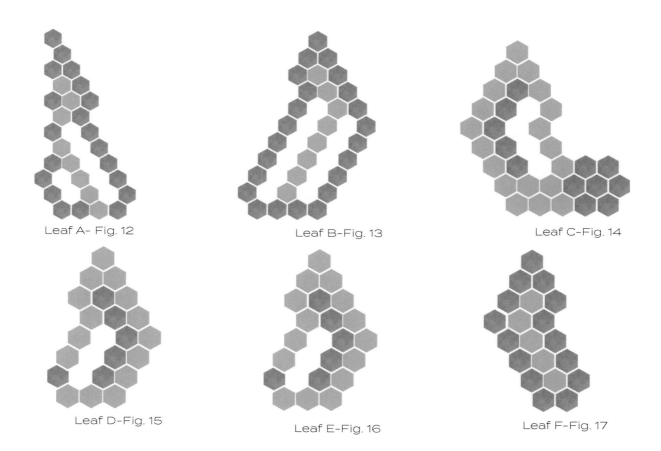

Leaf A- Fig. 12   Leaf B-Fig. 13   Leaf C-Fig. 14

Leaf D-Fig. 15   Leaf E-Fig. 16   Leaf F-Fig. 17

21. Apply side borders using a ¼" seam allowance; repeat with top and bottom borders. Press seams towards borders.

22. Quilt was quilted using assorted variegated thread. Swirls and ribbons were quilted in the stems and leaves. More swirls were quilted onto each tulip. I meandered in the background using light blue thread. The border was quilted using half of a feathered vine with pink variegated thread. See quilting diagram on page 38, as a reference.

Need a little pick me up? Try the lavender/olive oil soap on page 141..

Placement Diagram

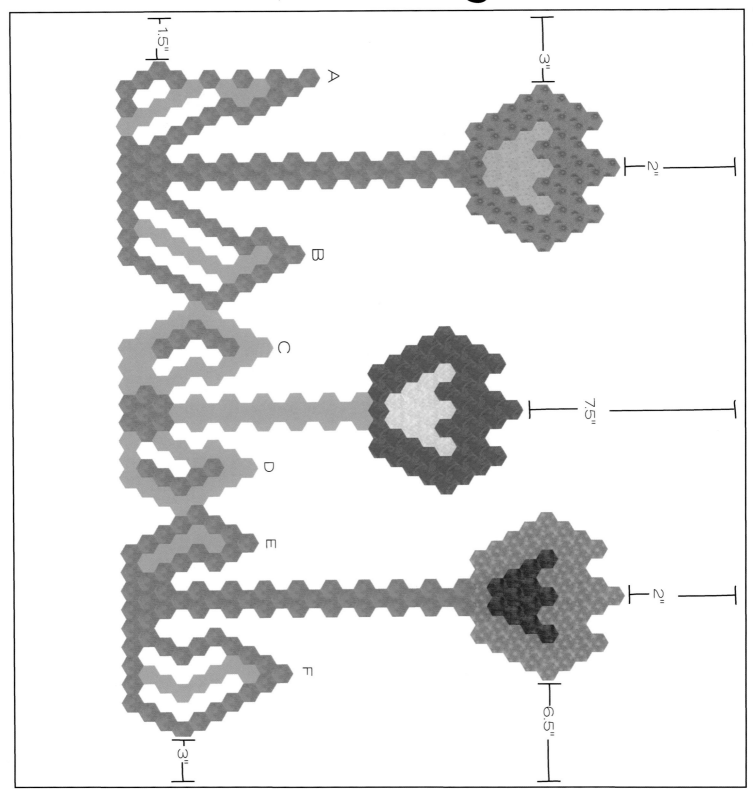

Quilting Diagram

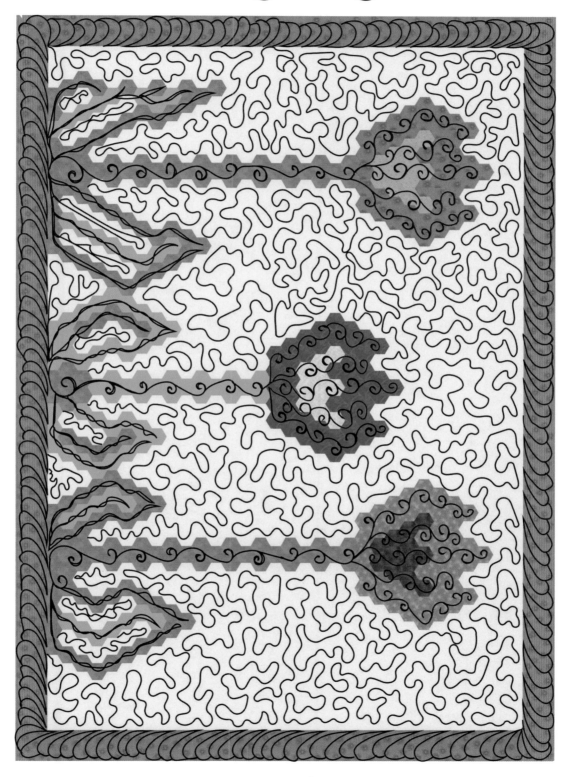

Under the Sea

Finished Tote Size 21"X 16.5"

A quilter can never have too many totes. These hexie fish are a swimmingly perfect way to store and carry all your quilting supplies.

Hexie Requirements (5/8")

 74 med green hexagons

 48 bright yellow hexagons

 41 dark blue hexagons

 107 bright pink hexagons

 102 med/dark red hexagons

 1 dark purple/red hexagons

Total number of hexagon foundations needed for this project: 373.

Materials

Yardage is based on 42" wide fabric

 3 yds light/med blue tonal batik-background and lining for bag

 ¼ yd medium green print

 ⅛ yd bright yellow print

 ¼ yd bright pink print

 ⅛ yd med/dark red solid

 ⅛ yd dark blue tonal

 Small scrap dark purple/red for large fish's eye

1½ yards medium blue batik for background, lining, pocket and straps. ¾ yard 48" wide muslin for backing. (This will be covered by the lining, and will not be visible.

Assembling the Quilt

Prepare the required number of each color hexagons, as per the instructions in the Prepping the Hexies section. (Page 13)

From medium blue batik cut:

(2) 42" X 17½"

(2) 17½" X 5"

(2) 4" X 32"

(1) 8½" X 15"

1. Join together (2) yellow hexies; repeat to make a total of (7) units.

2. Join together (2) blue hexies; repeat for a total of (8) units.

Fig. 1

3. Join a third yellow hexie to one of the yellow units made in step 1; repeat for a total of (2) units. (See Fig. 1)

Fig. 2

4. To one of the units made in step 3 add a fourth yellow hexie. (See Fig. 2)

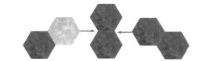

Fig. 3

5. Join together (1) blue hexie and (1) pink hexie. Join this unit and (2) of the double blue hexie units together. (See Fig. 3)

6. Join together (2) of the double yellow units to make one (4) hexie chain. Add (2) additional double units to the ends of this (4) hexie chain. (See Fig. 4)

Fig. 4

7. Stagger sew (6) of the double blue hexie units together. Add (1) yellow hexie to the top of this group. (See Fig. 5)

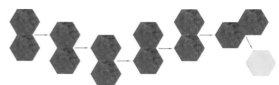

Fig. 5

8. Join together the units made in steps 1–8. (See Fig. 6)

9. Join (1) yellow hexie to (1) blue hexie. Attach this unit to one of the previously assembled (2) yellow units. (See Fig. 7)

10. Add the unit made in step 9 to the hexies assembled in step 8. (See Fig. 8)

11. Repeat steps 1–10 to make the second blue and yellow fish.

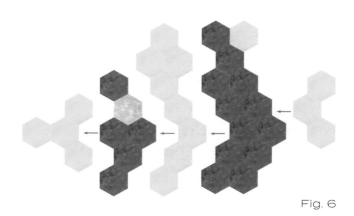

Fig. 6

Fig. 7

Big Fish Assembly

1. Combine (7) bright pink hexies to form one standard flower unit, as per the instructions in Sewing the Hexagons on page 18; repeat for a total of 4 units. (See Fig. 9)

2. Join together (2) red hexies; repeat (40) times. Join (1) additional red hexie to (16) of the double units. (See Fig. 10)

3. Combine two (2) hexie and two (3) hexie units to form Unit 1. (See Fig. 11 page 43)

4. Join together (2) bright pink hexies; repeat (33) times. Add an additional pink hexie to (6) of these units. Replicating the red units in pink (See Fig. 10)

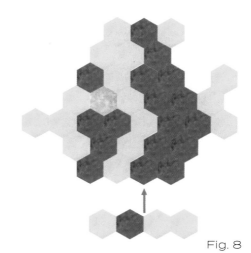

Fig. 8

Fig. 9

Fig. 10

5. Sew together (1) bright pink and (1) dark purple hexie.

6. Combine the pink/purple unit, (1) standard flower unit, (2) double pink units, one (3) pink unit, and one additional pink hexie to form Unit 2. (See Fig. 12)

7. Combine (4) double red units and (4) red (3) hexie units together to make Unit 3. (See Fig. 13)

8. Using (2) pink standard flower units, (6) double pink units, and one additional pink hexie, sew together to form Unit 4. (See Fig. 14)

9. Combine (5) red three hexie units with (2) red double hexie units to form Unit 5. (See Fig 15 page 44)

10. Sew together (12) double pink hexie units to form Unit 6. (See Fig. 16 page 44)

11. Combine (5) red three hexie units and (2) double red hexie units to form Unit 7. (See Fig. 17 page 44)

12. Sew together (1) pink three hexie unit and (9) pink double hexie units to form Unit 8. (See Fig. 18 page 44)

13. Combine (2) red double hexie units and one additional red hexie to form Unit 9. (See Fig. 19 page 44)

14. Using remaining triple pink hexie units and (1) additional pink hexie, sew together to form Unit 10. (See Fig. 20 page 44)

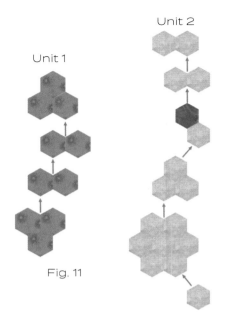

Unit 1

Unit 2

Fig. 11

Fig. 12

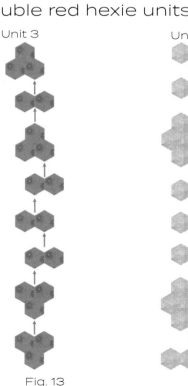

Unit 3

Unit 4

Fig. 13

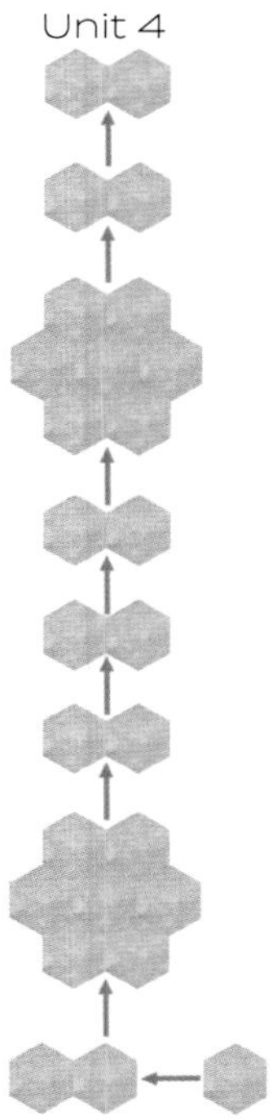

Fig. 14

Unit 5

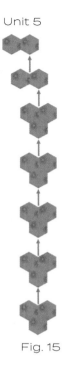

Fig. 15

Unit 6

Fig. 16

Unit 7

Fig. 17

Unit 8

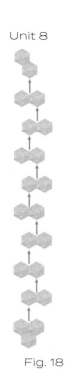

Fig. 18

Unit 9

Fig. 19

Unit 10

Fig. 20

15. Sew together the remaining pink standard flower unit and Units 1–10 to form body of large fish. (See Fig. 21)

16. Join together (5) red double hexie units to form a chain of (10).

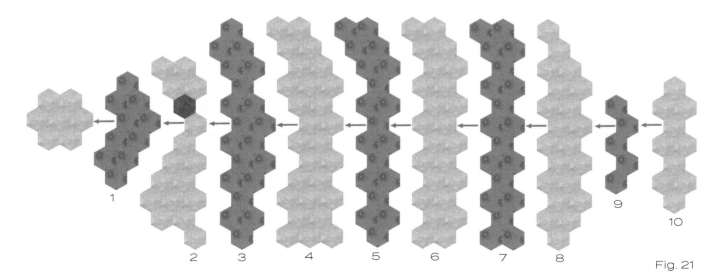

Fig. 21

17. Sew together (2) bright yellow hexies; repeat (3) times. Sew (1) dark blue hexie to one yellow hexie. Using (1) additional dark blue hexie, combine the double yellow units and the yellow/blue unit to form a long chain of hexies. Join this unit to the red (10) hexie chain made in step 16. (See Fig. 22)

18. Sew together (1) red and (1) yellow hexie; repeat (3) times. Sew together (2) blue hexies and (1) blue and (1) red hexie.

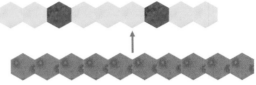

Fig. 22

19. Join (3) red double hexie units to make a chain of (6) hexies; repeat to make (2) chains (6) hexies long.

20. Join red/yellow units together alternating red/yellow units for a total of (6) hexies.

21. Add an additional red hexie to the red/blue unit. Join this to the end of the red/yellow unit made in the previous step. Hexies should go in order R/Y/R/Y/R/Y/R/B/R.

22. Join blue double hexie made previously to (1) of the red (6) hexie units. Add an additional double red hexie to the end of this unit following the double blue hexie unit. Join these three units together. (See Fig. 23)

23. Join sections made in steps 17-23 to bottom and top respectively of previously made fish body. (See Fig. 24)

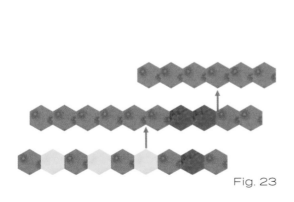

Fig. 23

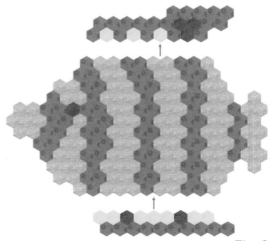

Fig. 24

24. Sew together (2) green hexies to make a double hexie unit; repeat for a total of (33) double units. Add (1) additional green hexie to (7) of these units to make (7) triple hexie chains. Using figures 25-30 as references, join these units together to form the seaweed.

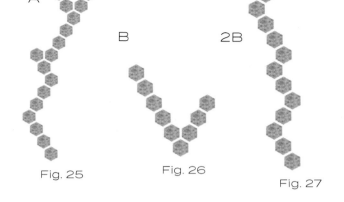

A

B   2B

Fig. 25   Fig. 26

Fig. 27

25. Apply a thin layer of glue to back of constructed units, and using placement guide on page 49 as a reference, glue to precut blue batik backing fabric. Heat set.

26. Using a narrow zig-zag stitch hexies to background fabric.

27. Quilt was quilted using a wavy water-like background filler. Ribbon candy was quilted in the seaweed and random wavy lines in fish for scales. I repeated the wavy water-like

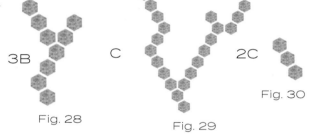

3B   C   2C

Fig. 30

Fig. 28   Fig. 29

background filler on one of the 17½" X 5" blue batik sections. (This will be the bottom of the bag) (See quilting diagram page 50.)

The pursuit, even of the best things, ought to be calm and tranquil.
Cicero

Bag Assembly

1. Trim the quilt to 42" X 17½" and the bottom section to 17½" X 5". Using a circle template (I used a 4" diameter circle) mark corners and trim. (See Fig. 1 & 2)

Fig. 1

Fig. 2

2. Bring together the short sides of the quilt, right sides together and sew together using a ½" seam allowance. Press open. (See Fig. 3)

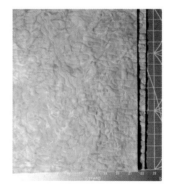

Fig. 3

3. Find the center of one of the long sides of the quilted bottom section and match this to the seam sewn in the previous step. Carefully pin the bottom piece to the quilt section gently easing to fit. Sew using a ½" seam allowance (See Fig. 4)

Fig. 4

4. Fold the 4" X 32" strip in half, right sides together, to make a 2" X 32" strip. Sew the long raw edges together using a ½" seam allowance. Do not sew short ends closed. Turn right side out; repeat to make second strap.

5. Pin raw edges of strap to top edge of right side of bag. Making sure not to twist straps. Repeat with second strap on opposite side of bag. Sew using a ¼" seam. Back stitch to reinforce.

6. Fold over one long edge of the 15½" X 8" section ¼" wrong sides together; press; turn under ¼" again; press. Sew close to turned edge. (This will be the top of the pocket.)

7. Fold under ¼" wrong sides together; on remaining (3) sides; press. Mark vertical lines on pocket from top to bottom starting on the left side at 2", 4", 6", and 12". (See Fig. 5)

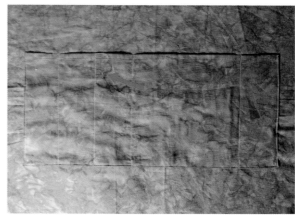

Fig. 5

8. Center on 42" X 17½" lining section lengthwise and 3" from the top. Wrong side to right side. Top-stitch close to the edge of the pocket on sides and bottom.

9. Sew along lines marked in step 34. Sewing from top to bottom of pocket to make partitions.

10. Repeat steps 2 & 3 using the dark blue batik lining sections. Note: When sewing the seam in step 2 leave open a 3" section for turning. (See Fig 6)

11. Right sides together, making sure straps are not caught in the seam, pin lining to bag. Sew using a ½" seam. Turn right side out through opening left in lining. Whip stitch opening closed.

Fig. 6

Placement Diagram

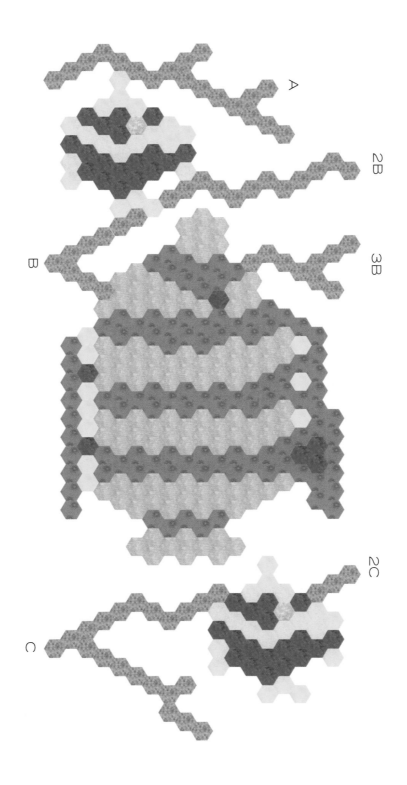

Quilting Diagram

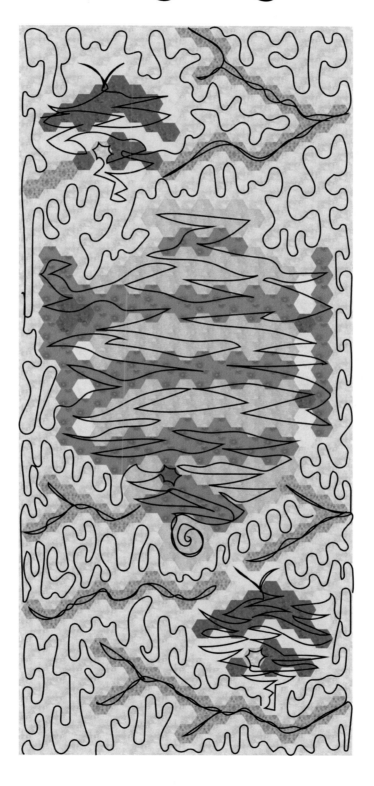

Up, Up, and Away

Finished quilt size 37" X 33"

Let your imagination soar with this bright and quirky wall hanging. Perfectly sized to add color and fun to any room..

Hexie Requirements (5⁄8")

 143 dark red hexagons

 110 dark blue hexagons

 38 brown/orange hexagons

 9 orange hexagons

 30 green hexagons

 24 purple hexagons

Total number of hexagon foundations needed for this project: 354.

Materials

Yardage is based on 42" wide fabric

 Fat quarter orange print

 ⅛ yd medium green print

 1 yd light blue

includes facing

 ⅛ yd purple tonal

 ⅜ yd med/dark blue print

 ⅜ yd red tonal

 ⅛ yd brown tonal

1 yd coordinating fabric of your choice for backing.

 We generate fears while we sit. We overcome them by action.
Dr. Henry Link

Assembling the Quilt

Prepare the required number of each color hexagons, as per the instructions in the Prepping the Hexies section. (Page 13)

From light blue fabric cut

(1) 33½" X 37½"

(2) 33½" X 2"

(2) 37" X 2"

You are never too old to set another goal or to dream a new dream.
C.S.. Lewis

Balloon A

1. Sew together a blue and a red hexie. Continue around the center hexagons to create the center standard flower, as per instructions in Sewing the Hexagons page 18. (See Fig. 1)

2. Continue adding hexagons to form additional rings to this base unit alternating red and blue rows referring to Fig. 2.

3. Join together (2) red hexagons. Repeat for a total of (23) double red units.

4. Join (2) of these double hexie units together and add one additional red hexie to the end to make a (5) hexie chain.

5. Continue joining double red hexagon units together to make the following units: 1- (8) hexie chain, 4- (6) hexie chain, and 1- (10) hexie chain.

Fig. 1

Fig. 2

6. Join together (2) blue hexies; repeat for a total of (17) double blue hexie units.

7. Join together (2) double blue units and add a single blue hexie to the end to make a (5) hexie chain; repeat for a total of (3) chains.

8. Join together double blue hexie units to make the following: 1- (4) hexie chain and 2- (8) hexie chain. Join the (4) hexie chain to one of the (5) hexie chains made in the previous step to make 1- (9) hexie chain. Join (1) double hexie unit to another of the (5) hexie chains to make 1- (7) hexie chain.

9. Join units made in the previous steps to the center unit made in step 2 using Fig. 3 as a guide.

10. Join together (2) bright orange hexies; repeat for a total of (2) double units. Add (1) extra hexie to the end of one of these double units. Join (1) double orange hexie unit to the triple chain. (See Fig. 4)

11. Join together (2) brown hexies to form a double brown unit; repeat for a total of (12) units.

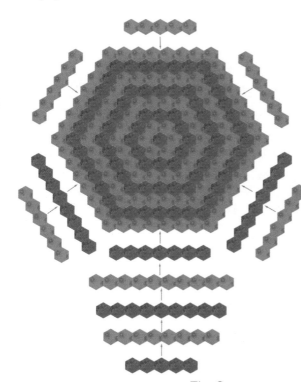

Fig. 3

Fig. 4

Take a minute to unwind and just be in the moment with these yoga poses- Warrior 2 & Dolphin on page 135 & 136.

Balloon A-continued

12. Add (1) extra brown hexie to (6) of the double brown hexie units to make 6-(3) hexie chains. Join (1) double brown unit to (1) triple unit; repeat. (See Fig. 5)

13. Join (2) triple brown hexie units together to make 1- (6) hexie chain. Add (1) double unit to a triple unit to make 1- (5) hexie chain. Join (2) double units together to create 1- (4) hexie chain. Join units made in steps 12 & 13 together to form balloon basket. (See Fig. 6)

14. Join basket and flame to balloon. (See Fig. 7)

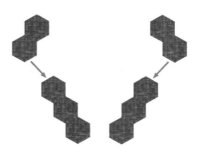

Fig. 5

Fig. 7

Fig. 6

 Take time to unwind and treat yourself to one of these decadent night creams on page 143-144.

Balloon B

1. Join together (3) green hexies as per Fig. 1

2. Sew a row of purple hexagons around the unit made in step 1. (See Fig. 2)

3. Sew an additional row of green hexies around the unit made in step 2. (See Fig. 3)

4. Join together (2) brown hexies; repeat to make (2) double brown units. Add (1) additional brown unit to (1) of the double units to make (1) triple unit. Join together (2) bright orange hexies to make a double orange hexie unit.

5. Sew together the unit made in step 3, the double orange and brown units and the triple brown unit made in step 4. (See Fig. 4)

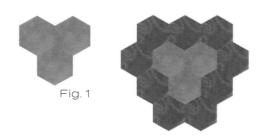

Fig. 1

Fig. 2

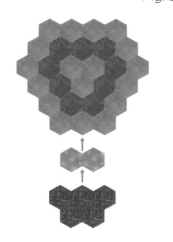

Fig. 3

Fig. 4

 You've gotta dance like there's nobody watching, love like you'll never be hurt, sing like there's nobody listening, and live like it's heaven on earth.
William W. Purkey

Balloon C

1. Join together (2) green hexies; repeat to make (5) double green hexie units.

2. Join together (2) purple hexies; repeat to make (7) double purple units.

3. Using Fig. 1-5 as reference join these units with the remaining single purple and green units to form the stripes of the balloon.

4. Join together (2) brown hexies; repeat to make (2) double brown units. Add (1) additional brown unit to (1) of the double units to make (1) triple unit. Join together (2) bright orange hexies to make a double orange hexie unit.

5. Sew together the unit made in step 3, the double orange and brown units and the triple brown unit made in step 4. (See Fig. 6 page 58)

6. Apply a thin layer of glue to the backs of the balloons and using the placement guide on page 59 as a reference, position them on the 33½"X 37½" blue background fabric.

7. Quilt was quited using a swirling wind-like background filler. Continuous curves were quilted in the baskets, and swirls and loops in the balloons. See the quilting guide on page 60 as a reference.

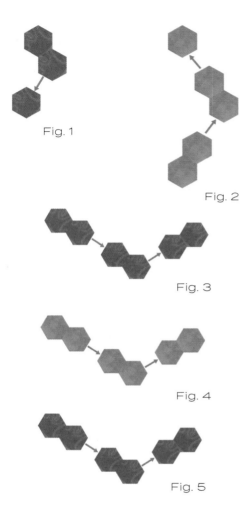

Fig. 1

Fig. 2

Fig. 3

Fig. 4

Fig. 5

8. A facing was applied instead of a binding to create the appearance of an uninterrupted sky. (See *Stress Free Quilting*™ Borders, Bindings, and More for facing instructions and other creative ways to finish your quilts.)

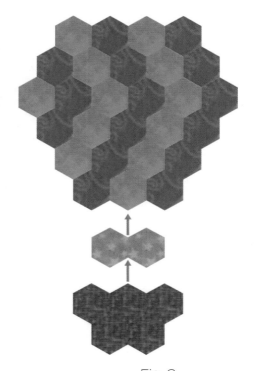

Fig. 6

Let your worries drift away while enjoying a relaxing herbal bath with this luxurious rose and almond facial scrub page 145-146.

Don't limit yourself. Many people limit themselves to what they think they can do. You can go as far as your mind lets you. What you believe, remember, you can achieve.
Mary Kay Ash

Placement Diagram

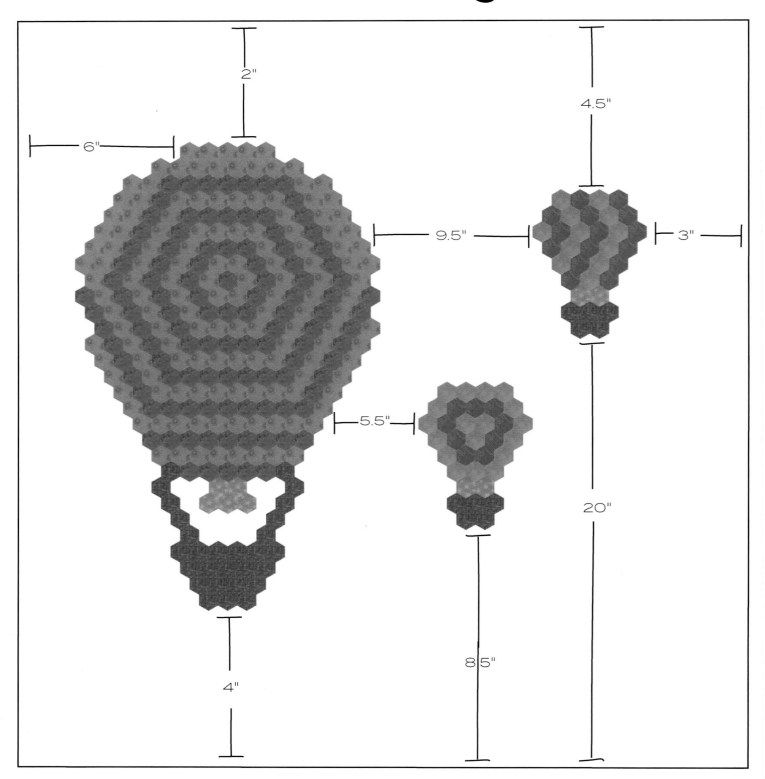

Quilting Diagram

Flutterby, Butterfly

Finished quilt size 33½" X 32"

Let your sense of color fly free with this whimsical butterfly quilt.

Hexie Requirements (5/8")

 122 red tonal hexagons

 160 purple batik hexagons

 92 medium blue hexagons

 42 bright yellow hexagons

 30 medium brown hexagons

Total number of hexagon foundations needed for this project: 446.

Materials

Yardage is based on 42" wide fabric

 1 yd medium blue

includes borders and binding

 1 yd light blue

 ⅜ yd purple batik

 ⅜ yd red tonal/batik

 ⅛ yd bright yellow

 ⅛ yd medium brown

1 yd coordinating fabric of your choice for backing.

 All things are difficult, before they are easy...
Thomas Fuller

Assembling the Quilt

Prepare the required number of each color hexagons, as per the instructions in the Prepping the Hexies section. (Page 13)

From light blue fabric cut

(1) 27½" X 29"

From medium blue print cut

(2) 2½" X 27½"

(2) 2½" X 33½"

---

1. Join together bright yellow hexies to form (2) standard flower units, as per instructions in Sewing the Hexagons on page 18. Join together (2) additional yellow hexies to form a double hexie unit; repeat for a total of (10) double yellow units.

2. Join together (2) of the double units to form a (4) hexie chain; repeat to make (4)- (4) hexie chains.

3. Add an additional yellow hexie to the (2) remaining double yellow units to make (2) triple yellow hexie units.

4. Add (2) additional yellow hexies as per Fig. 1 and 2 to each standard flower unit. (Figures show mirror images for Left & Right wings)

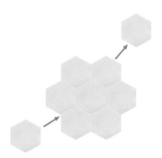

Fig. 1

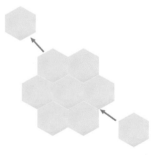

Fig. 2

5. Join one of the (4) hexie chains to the bottom of each of the units made in step 4. (See Figs. 3 and 4)

6. Join together (2) medium blue hexies; repeat to make (2) double blue hexie units. Add an additional blue hexie to each of these units. (See Fig. 5)

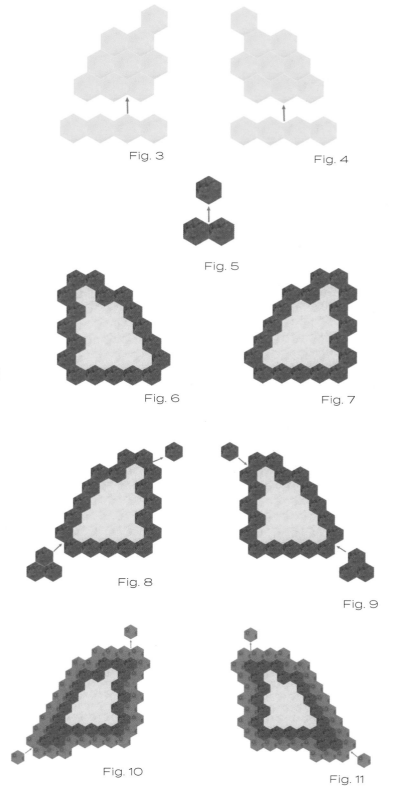

Fig. 3

Fig. 4

Fig. 5

7. Attach blue hexies to the outside of each of the yellow units made in step 5 using the same method as you used to make a standard flower. (See Figs. 6 & 7)

Fig. 6

Fig. 7

8. Join one of the units made in step 6 to the unit made in the previous step. Join an additional blue hexie to the top of this unit. Repeat with the other unit. (See Fig. 8 & 9)

9. Sew a row of red hexies around each of the units made in the previous step using the method used to make a standard flower unit. Add an additional red hexie to the top and bottom of each unit. (See Figs. 10 & 11)

Fig. 8

Fig. 9

Fig. 10

Fig. 11

10. Continuing in the same manner; sew a row of purple hexies around the units made in step 9. NOTE that this row does not go all the way around! Add (1) additional purple hexie to the side of this unit; repeat with the other wing. (See Figs. 12 & 13)

Fig. 12

Fig. 13

11. Join together (1) of the triple yellow hexie chains to (1) of the (4) yellow hexie chains made in steps 2 & 3. Add an additional yellow hexie to this unit. (See Figs. 14 & 15)

Fig. 14

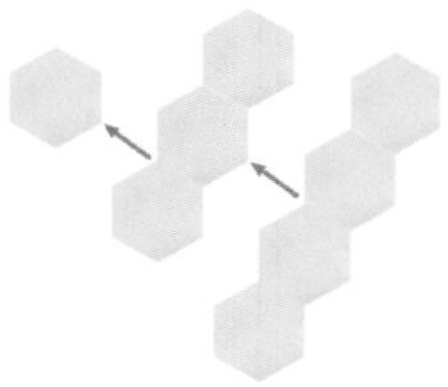

Fig. 15

12. Sew a row of purple hexies around each of these units adding (2) additional purple hexies as per Figs. 16 & 17.

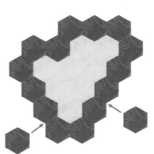

Fig. 16

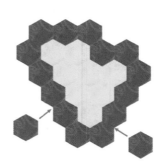

Fig. 17

13. Next sew a row of blue hexies around the purple hexies added in the previous step. Add (2) additional blue hexies as per Figs. 18 & 19.

14. Sew a row of red hexies around the previously added blue hexies adding (1) additional red hexie to each unit. (See Figs. 20 & 21 on page 66)

Fig. 19

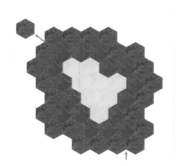

Fig. 18

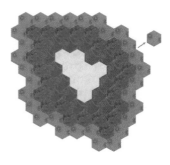

Fig. 21   Fig. 20

15. Next add a row of purple hexies to each unit. NOTE that this row will not go all the way around! Add (1) additional purple hexie to each unit. (See Figs. 22 & 23)

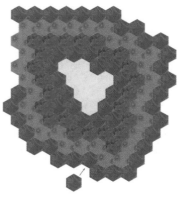

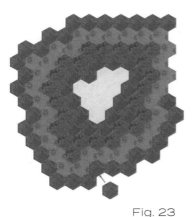

Fig. 22   Fig. 23

16. Join together (2) brown hexies; repeat for a total of (11) units. Join (2) of the double brown units together to make a (4) hexie chain. Add (1) additional brown hexie to (5) of these double brown units. (See Fig. 24)

Fig. 24

17. Join together (5) of these units to make a chain. (See Fig. 25)

18. Add an additional hexie to the top of this chain. (See Fig. 26)

19. Join (1) brown hexie to (1) of the double brown units; repeat to make (2) of these units. (See Fig. 27)

20. Join the unit made in the previous step to one of (4) hexie chains made in step 16; repeat. (See Figs. 28 & 29) (Again these are mirror images for the Left and Right antennae)

21. Join the units made in step 20 to the chain made in step 18. (See Fig. 30)

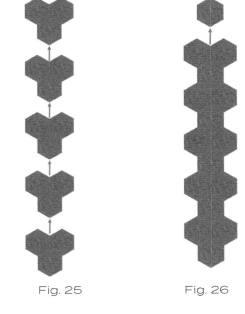

Fig. 25   Fig. 26

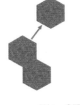

Fig. 27

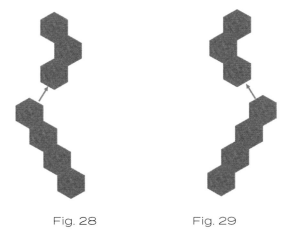

Fig. 28   Fig. 29

Fig. 30

22. Join Left Upper Wing to Left Lower Wing; Repeat with Right Upper and Lower Wing. (See Fig 31 & 32)

23. Join left and right wing units to center body. (See Fig. 33)

24. Apply a thin layer of glue to the back of the butterfly, and using the placement diagram on page 69, as a guide, center the butterfly on the light blue backing fabric.

25. Apply dark blue borders to sides of quilt using a ¼" seam allowance. Press seam towards border. Repeat with top and bottom borders.

26. Quilt was quilted with a swirling pattern in the borders, and a looping meander was used in the background. The butterfly was quilted with swirls in the body and alternating swirls and loops in the wings. (See Quilting Diagram on page 70)

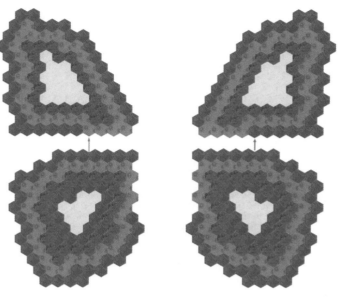

Fig. 31   Fig. 32

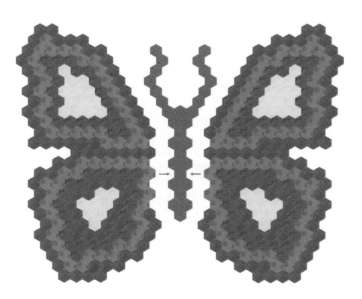

Fig. 33

Placement Diagram

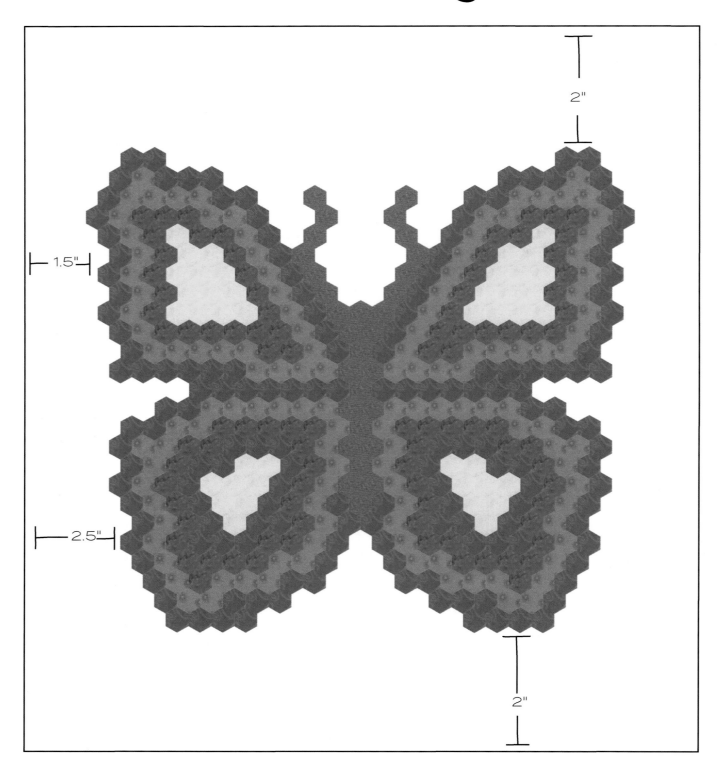

Quilting Diagram

Bargello De Hexagons

Finished Quilt Size 51" X 35"

This lap quilt/wall hanging is a fun new take on a bargello quilt and is sure to brighten up any room

Hexie Requirements (1")

 80 dark blue batik hexagons

 36 lavender hexagons

 44 light pink hexagons

 14 med. blue batik hexagons

 68 cream hexagons

 39 med. purple print hexagons

 28 dark purple hexagons

 42 lt. purple print hexagons

 46 lt. turquoise hexagons

 52 red print hexagons

 66 beige print hexagons

Total number of hexagon foundations needed for this project: 615.

Materials

Yardage is based on 42" wide fabric

 ¼ yd red print

 ¼ yd light pink print

 ¼ yd lavender print

 ½ yd medium blue batik

 ⅜ yd beige/tan print

 ¼ yd light turquoise

 ⅜ cream tone on tone

 1½ yds dark blue batik

includes borders and binding

 ¼ light purple print

 ⅛ yd dark purple print

 ¼ yd medium purple print

Assembling the Quilt

Prepare the required number of each color hexagons, as per the instructions in the Prepping the Hexies section. (Page 13)

From dark purple batik cut:

(2)- 2½" X 31½"

(2)- 2½" X 51½"

For an invigorating start to your day, try the citrus body scrub on page 142.

Center Unit

1. Starting with a medium purple hexie, sew lavender hexies around it to create a standard flower, as per instructions in Sewing the Hexagons on page 18 (See Fig. 1)

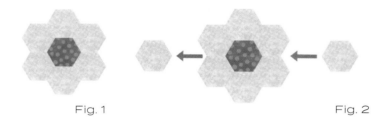

Fig. 1   Fig. 2

2. Join (1) additional lavender hexie to each side of the unit made in step 1. (See Fig. 2)

3. Join together (2) light purple hexies to make a double hexie unit; repeat for a total of (6) units.

4. Join (2) of the light purple double units together to make a (4) hexie unit; repeat for a total of (2) units. Join an additional light purple hexie to the end of (2) of the double units to make two (3) hexie chains..

5. Add a medium purple hexie to the end of each of the (3) light purple hexie chains. (See Fig. 3)

Fig. 3

6. Join the units made in steps 4 & 5 to the unit made in step 2. (See Fig. 4)

7. Join together (2) dark purple hexies; repeat for a total of (6) units. Join (2) of the double hexies together to make a (4) hexie chain: repeat to make (2) chains. Add an additional dark purple hexie to (2) of the double units to make two (3) hexie chains.

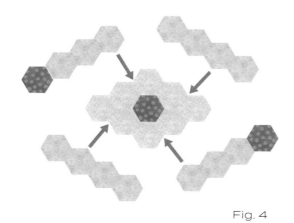

Fig. 4

8. Join together (2) light purple units to make a double hexie unit; repeat for a total of (4) units.

9. Join (1) of the double light purple units to (1) of the (3) dark purple hexie chains and add an additional dark purple hexie to the end of this chain; repeat for a total of (2) units. (See Fig. 5)

10. Join (1) of the dark purple (4) hexie chains to (1) of the double light purple units; repeat to make (2) of these (6) hexie chains. (See Fig. 6)

Fig. 5

11. Join the units made in steps 9 & 10 to the unit made in step 6. (See Fig. 7)

12. Join together (2) dark purple hexies to make a double hexie unit; repeat for a total of (4) units. Add an additional dark purple hexie to the end of each of these units to make four (3) hexie chains.

Fig. 6

13. Join together (2) turquoise hexies to make a double hexie unit; repeat for a total of (8) double units. Join together (2) of these units to make a (4) hexie chain; repeat for a total of (2) chains. Add an additional turquoise hexie to the end of each of the remaining double units to make two (3) hexie chains.

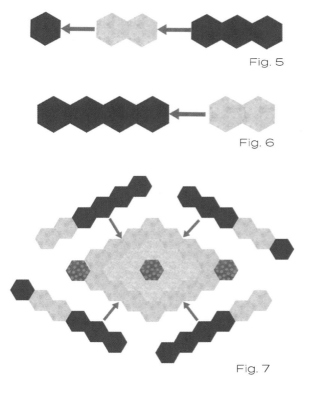

Fig. 7

14. Join together (1) double turquoise unit, (1) triple dark purple chain, and (1) triple turquoise chain; repeat to make a total of (2) units. (See Fig. 8)

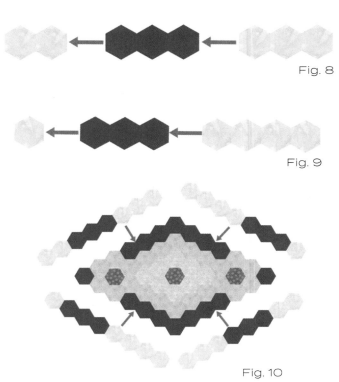

Fig. 8

15. Join together (1) triple dark purple chain, (1) additional turquoise hexie, and (1) of the quadruple turquoise chains; repeat for a total of (2) units. (See Fig. 9)

Fig. 9

16. Join the units made in step 14 & 15 to the unit made in step 11. (See Fig 10)

17. Join together (2) turquoise hexies to make a double hexie unit; repeat for a total of (12) units. Join these together to make four (6) hexie chains.

Fig. 10

18. Join together (2) medium blue hexies to make a double hexie unit. Add an additional blue hexie to make a (3) hexie chain; repeat for a total of (4) triple chains.

19. Join together (1) of the turquoise (6) hexie chains, (1) triple blue chain and (1) additional blue hexie; repeat for a total of (2) units. (See Fig. 11)

20. Join together (1) of the turquoise (6) hexie chains, (1) triple blue chain and (1) additional turquoise hexie; repeat for a total of (2) units. (See Fig. 12)

21. Sew the units made in steps 19 & 20 to the unit made in step 16. (See Fig. 13 page 76)

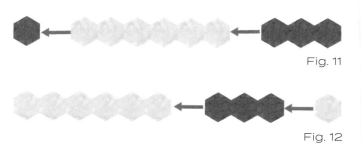

Fig. 11

22. Join together (2) dark blue hexies to make a double unit; repeat for a total of (4) units

Fig. 12

23. Join together (2) medium blue hexies to make a double unit; repeat for a total of (16) units. Join these units together to make four chains of (8) hexies each. Add (1) additional medium blue hexie to the end of (2) of these chains to make (2) units of (9) hexies each.

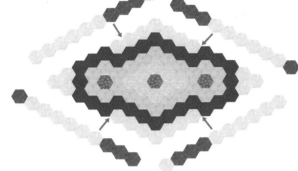

Fig. 13

24. Sew (1) dark blue (2) hexie unit, (1) medium blue (2) hexie unit and (1) medium blue (8) hexie chain together; repeat for a total of (2) units. (See Fig. 14)

25. Sew together (1) dark blue double hexie unit, (1) medium blue (9) hexie chain and (1) additional medium blue hexie; repeat for a total of (2) units. (See Fig. 15)

26. Join the units made in steps 24 & 25 to the sides of the unit made in step 21. (See Fig. 16)

Fig. 14

27. Join together (2) dark blue hexies; repeat for a total of (24) double units. Join (5) of these units together to form a 10 hexie chain; repeat for a total of (4) of these units. Add (1) additional unit to (2) of these units to make two chains (11) hexies long.

Fig. 15

28. Add an additional dark blue hexie to (2) of the remaining units to make (2) triple hexie chains.

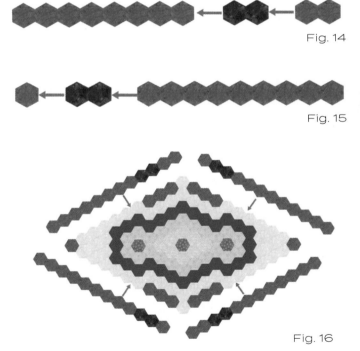

Fig. 16

29. Join (1) dark blue (10) hexie chain, (1) cream hexie, and (1) triple dark blue chain; repeat to make a total of (2) units. (See Fig. 17)

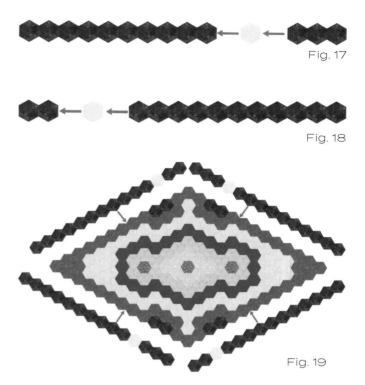

Fig. 17

Fig. 18

30. Join together (1) double dark blue unit, (1) cream hexie, and (1) dark blue (11) hexie chain; repeat for a total of (2) units. (See Fig. 18)

31. Sew the units made in steps 29 & 30 to the unit made in step 26. (See Fig. 19)

Fig. 19

Right Upper and Left Lower Corner Unit

To make the right upper and left lower corner units sew together (2) of each of the following hexie chains:
(3) dark blue hexies
(5) light purple hexies
(7) lavender hexies
(9) medium purple hexies
(11) pink hexies
(13) red hexies
(15) medium blue
(16) cream hexies
(17) beige hexies

Surround yourself with people who believe in your dreams, encourage your ideas, support your ambitions, and bring out the best in you...
Roy Bennett

1. Join (1) additional dark blue hexie to the dark blue (3) hexie chain. (See Fig. 1)

Fig. 1

Fig. 2

2. Join this unit to the light purple (5) hexie chain. (See Fig. 2)

3. Add the lavender (7) hexie chain. (See Fig. 3)

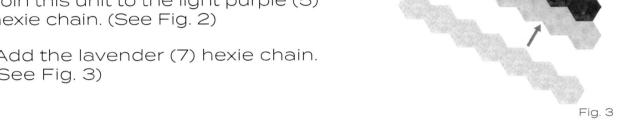

Fig. 3

4. To this unit, add the medium purple (9) hexie chain. (See Fig. 4)

5. Continue by adding the pink (11) hexie chain. (See Fig. 5)

6. To this unit add the red (13) hexie chain. (See Fig. 6)

Fig. 4

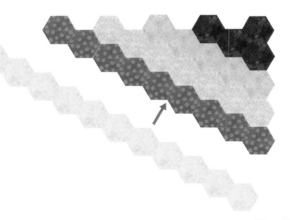

Fig. 5

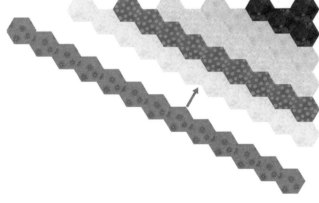

Fig. 6

7. To this unit, add the medium blue (15) hexie chain. (See Fig. 7)

8. Next add the beige (17) hexie chain. (See Fig. 8)

9. To finish this unit add the cream (16) hexie chain. (See Fig. 9)

10. Repeat steps 1-9 to make a total of (2) corner units.

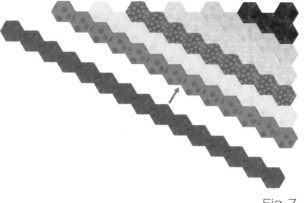

Fig. 7

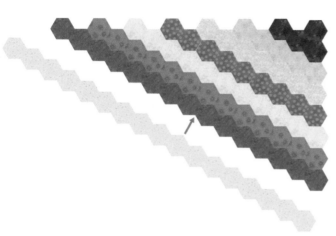

Fig. 8

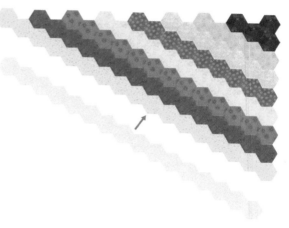

Fig. 9

Left Upper and Right Lower Corner Unit

To make the right upper and left lower corner units sew together (2) of each of the following hexie chains:
(3) dark blue hexies
(5) light purple hexies
(7) lavender hexies
(9) medium purple hexies
(11) pink hexies
(13) red hexies
(15) medium blue
(16) beige hexies
(16) cream hexies

Extended triangle pose on page 140 is a great way to unwind and relax.

1. Join (1) additional dark blue hexie to the dark blue (3) hexie chain. (See Fig. 1)

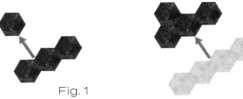

Fig. 1

Fig. 2

2. Join this unit to the light purple (5) hexie chain. (See Fig. 2)

3. Add the Lavender (7) hexie chain. (See Fig. 3)

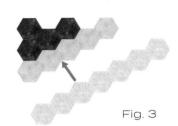

Fig. 3

4. To this unit, add the medium purple (9) hexie chain. (See Fig. 4)

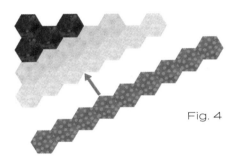

Fig. 4

5. Continue by adding the pink (11) hexie chain. (See Fig. 5)

6. To this unit add the red (13) hexie chain. (See Fig. 6)

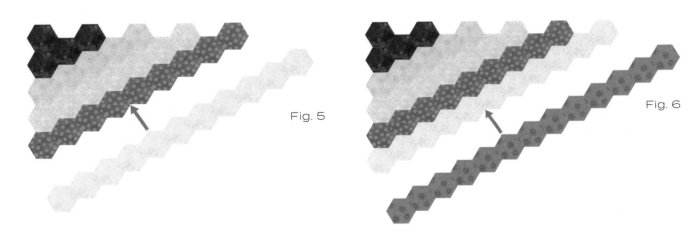

Fig. 5

Fig. 6

7. To this unit, add the medium blue (15) hexie chain. (See Fig. 7)

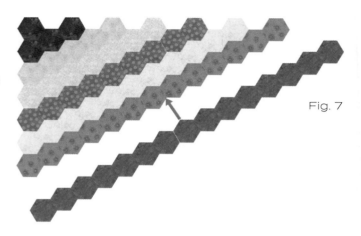

Fig. 7

8. Next add the beige (16) hexie chain. (See Fig. 8)

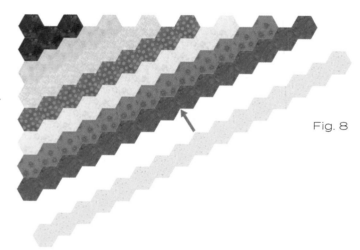

Fig. 8

9. To finish this unit add the cream (16) hexie chain. (See Fig. 9)

10. Repeat steps 1–9 to make a total of (2) corner units.

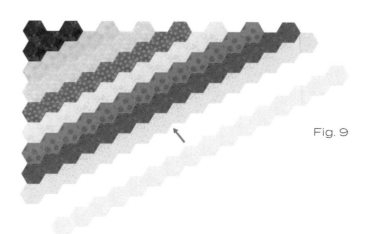

Fig. 9

Assembling the Quilt

Starting with the Right Upper Corner, and working clockwise, add the corner units to the center unit. See Figure 10 and placement diagram on page 83 for reference.

Fig. 10

Quilt was quilted using a combination of continuous curves, loops and swirls. I used a medium taupe colored thread to blend with all the different colors. See Quilting Diagram on page 84 for reference.

Placement Diagram

Quilting Diagram

Diamonds Are A Girl's Best Friend

Finished Quilt Size 66½" X 82½"

Diamonds are indeed a quilter's best friend in this fun quilt using modern hexies to achieve a traditional vibe.

Hexie Requirements (1")

 276 med/dk purple hexagons

 256 medium blue hexagonS

 164 medium green hexagons

 302 med/dark gray hexagons

 236 light purple hexagons

Total number of hexagon foundations needed for this project: 1234.

Materials

Yardage is based on 42" wide fabric

 3½ yds med/dark purple
batik includes borders and binding

 2½ yds medium blue tonal includes borders

 1 yd medium green tonal

 1⅜ yds light purple

 1¾ yds dark gray

2½ yds coordinating 108 wide fabric for backing, or 5½ yds of 42" wide. (Seam will run vertically to the quilt top.)

 If sitting too long is making your back ache, try the Locust pose on page 138.

Assembling the Quilt

Prepare the required number of each color hexagons, as per the instructions in the Prepping the Hexies section. (Page 13)

From blue fabric cut:

(2) 2" X 57½"

(2) 2" X 77"

From purple fabric cut

(2) 3½" X 61"

(2) 3½" X 83½"

Believe in yourself!.. Have faith in your abilities!.. Without a humble but reasonable confidence in your own powers, you cannot be successful or happy... Norman Vincent Peale

Center Diamond Unit

1. Using the method described in Sewing the Hexies (page 18), start with a dark purple hexie and create a standard flower unit by surrounding it with green hexies. (See Fig. 1)

2. Add a row of light purple hexies to this unit. (See Fig. 2)

3. Add a third row of dark gray and light purple hexies to unit. (See Fig. 3)

Fig. 1

Fig. 2

Fig. 3

4. Join together (2) dark gray hexies add an additional dark gray hexie to this double unit; repeat (See Fig. 4)

Fig. 4

5. Join one light purple hexie to one dark gray hexie. Add an additional dark gray hexie to the other side of the light purple hexie. Join this triple hexie chain to the unit made in step 4; repeat. (See Fig. 5)

Fig. 5

6. Add the (2) units made in the previous step to the top and bottom of the standard flower unit made in step 2. (See Fig. 6)

7. Repeat steps 1-6 to make a total of (6) center diamond units

Blue Diamond Unit

1. Using the method described in Sewing the Hexies (page 18), start with a green hexie and create a standard flower unit by surrounding it with blue and green hexies. (See Fig. 1)

Fig. 6

Fig. 1

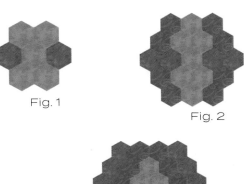

Fig. 2

2. Add a row of purple, green, and blue hexies to this unit. (See Fig. 2)

3. Add a row of purple, and blue hexies to this unit. (See Fig. 3)

Fig. 3

4. Join together (2) blue hexies, add an additional blue hexie to this unit. (See Fig. 4)

5. Sew together (1) purple and (1) blue hexie. Add an additional blue hexie to the other side of the purple hexie. Join this chain to the unit made in step 4; repeat. See Fig. 5)

6. Add the units made in step 5 to the top and the bottom of the standard flower unit completed in step 3; repeat steps 1-6 to make a total of (6) blue diamond units (See Fig. 6)

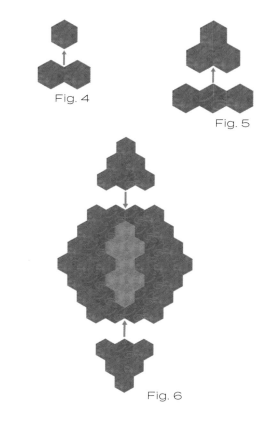

Fig. 4

Fig. 5

Fig. 6

Purple Diamond Unit

1. Using the method described in Sewing the Hexies (page 18), start with a green hexie and create a standard flower unit by surrounding it with purple and green hexies. (See Fig. 1)

2. Add a row of purple, green, and blue hexies to this unit. (See Fig. 2)

3. Add a row of purple, and blue hexies to this unit. (See Fig. 3)

4. Join together (2) purple hexies, add an additional purple hexie to this unit. (See Fig. 4)

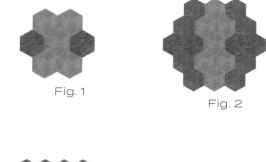

Fig. 1

Fig. 2

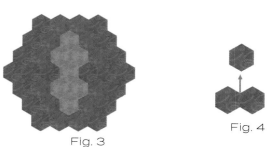

Fig. 3

Fig. 4

5. Sew together (1) purple and (1) blue hexie. Add an additional purple hexie to the other side of the blue hexie. Join this chain to the unit made in step 4; repeat. (See Fig. 5)

6. Add the units made in step 5 to the top and the bottom of the standard flower unit completed in step 3; repeat steps 1-6 to make a total of (6) purple diamond units (See Fig. 6)

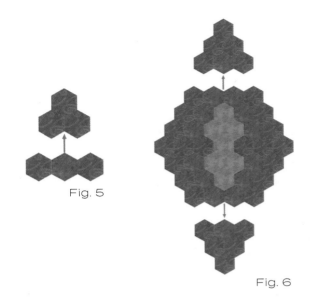

Fig. 5

Fig. 6

Top/Bottom Diamonds

1. Join together (1) gray and (1) light purple hexie. Add an additional gray hexie to this unit; repeat for a total of (12) units. (See Fig. 1)

2. Join together (2) dark gray hexies. Add an additional gray hexie to this unit; repeat for a total of (6) units. (See Fig. 2)

3. Starting with a light purple hexie add light purple and green hexies to make a standard flower unit. (See Fig. 3)

4. Use green, light purple, dark purple, and gray hexies to make the next row of this unit. (See Fig. 4)

5. Join the units made in step 1 & 2 to the sides of the unit made in the previous step; repeat Steps 3-5 to make a total of (6) Side Diamond Units.. (See Fig 5)

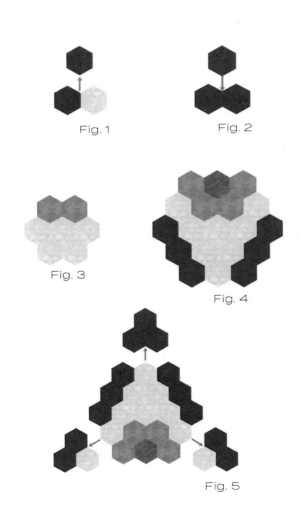

Fig. 1

Fig. 2

Fig. 3

Fig. 4

Fig. 5

Corner Diamond Units

1. Join together a chain of (7) gray hexies; repeat for a total of (4) gray units.

2. Join together a chain of (5) light purple hexies; repeat for a total of (4) units

3. Join together (2) green hexies, add an additional light purple hexie to the end of this unit; repeat for a total of (4) units.

4. Join these rows together as per Figs. 1-4. (Note these units are directional and each is specific to its own corner.)

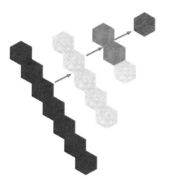

Fig. 1-Upper Right Corner

Fig. 2-Upper Left Corner

Fig. 3- Bottom Right Corner

Fig. 4-Bottom Left Corner

Side Diamond Units

1. Starting with a green hexie make a standard flower unit using light purple, green and dark purple hexies. (See Fig. 1)

Fig. 1

2. Join together (3) dark gray hexies as per Fig. 2.

3. Join the units made in step 1 and 2 together as per Fig. 3.

4. Next join together a chain of (5) gray hexies and a chain of (3) light purple hexies. Using these and (1) additional light purple hexie, join together to form the unit in Fig. 4. Repeat to make (2) of these units.

5. Join together the units made in the previous step with the unit made in step 3. (See Fig. 5)

6. Repeat steps 1-6 to make a total of (6) Side Diamond Units.

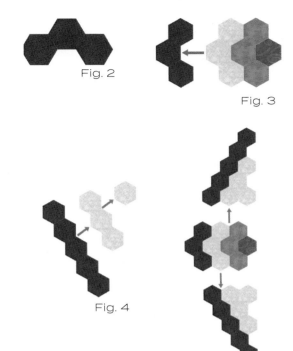

Fig. 2

Fig. 3

Fig. 4

Fig. 5

Assembling The Quilt

1. Join together (1) top diamond, (1) blue diamond and (1) side diamond unit. (See Fig. 1)

2. To this section, add Upper Right Corner Unit. (See Fig. 2 on page 93)

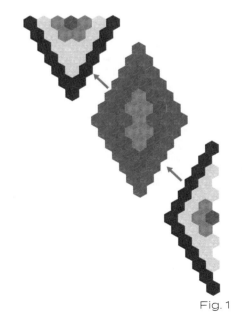

Fig. 1

3. Next join together: (1) top/bottom, (2) purple diamonds, (1) center diamond, and (1) side diamond unit. (See Fig. 3)

Fig. 2

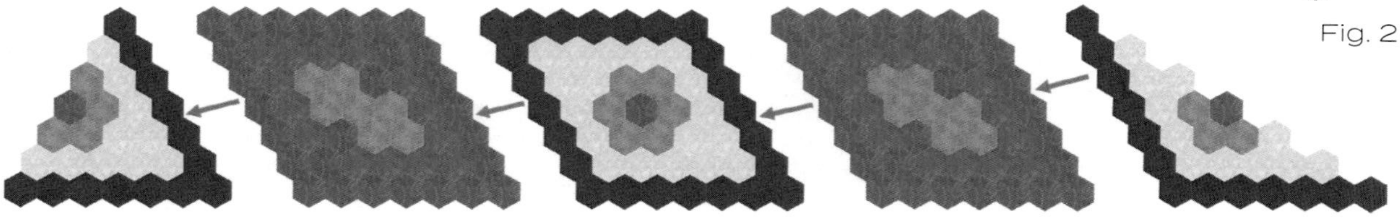

Fig. 3

4. For the next row, join together: (1) top/bottom diamond unit, (2) center diamond units, (3) blue diamond units, and Right Lower Corner Unit. (See Fig. 4)

Fig. 4

5. To make the next row, join together; (1) top/bottom diamond, (2) center diamond units, (3) purple diamond units, and Left Upper Corner Unit. (See Fig. 5 page 94)

Fig. 5

6. For the next row, join together: (1) top/bottom diamond unit, (2) blue diamonds units, and (1) side diamond unit. (See Fig. 6)

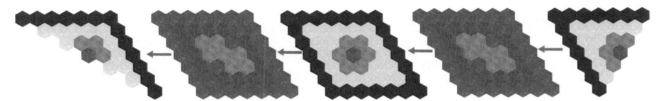

Fig. 6

7. Join together (1) top/bottom diamond. (1) purple diamond unit and (1) side diamond unit. (See Fig 7)

8. Add the Left Bottom Corner unit to the unit made in step 6. (See Fig. 8)

Fig. 7

Fig. 8

9. Join rows made in steps 1-7 together to form the quilt top. (See Fig. 9) See placement diagram on page 96, as a reference.

Fig. 9

Quilt was quilted using a swirl design in the outer border and loops in the inner border. Feathers were quilted in the green hexagon flowers with a combination of filigree work and continuous curves quilted in the blue and purple diamonds. See quilting design on page 97.

Placement Diagram

Quilting Diagram

Variation

Star Brite

Total number of hexagon foundations needed for this project: 1827.

Finished Quilt Size 79" X 82"

Hexie Requirements (1")

 112 dark purple hexies

 12 medium purple hexies

 68 light purple hexies

 110 dark blue hexies

 14 medium blue hexies

 73 light blue hexies

 103 dark green hexies

 12 medium green hexies

 72 light green hexies

 94 dark red hexies

 67 medium red hexies

 11 medium pink hexies

 90 dark orange hexies

 58 medium orange hexies

 11 bright yellow hexies

 554 dark brown hexies

366 cream hexies

Materials

Yardage is based on 42" wide fabric

 ⅝ yd dark purple print

 ⅛ yd med. purple print

 2½ yds lt. purple print includes fabric for borders and binding

 ⅝ yd dark blue print

 ⅛ yd medium blue print

 ½ yd light blue print

 ⅝ yd dark green print

 ⅛ yd med. green print

 ⅜ yd light green print

 ½ yd dark red print

 ⅜ yd medium red print

 ⅛ yd medium pink print

 ½ yd dark orange print

 ⅜ yd med. orange print

 ⅛ yd bright yellow print

 2¾ yds dark brown

 1⅞ yds cream

Star lite star brite, hexies in the sky with diamonds. This fun traditional hexie quilt will brighten any bedroom, and can easily be modified to fit your color scheme.

Prepare the required number of each color hexagons, as per the instructions in the Prepping the Hexies section. (Page 13)

Additional fabric needed: 2⅓ yds coordinating fabric for backing.

Cut from light purple:

(2) 2" by approximately 86"

(2) 2¼" by approximately 83"

Diamond Units

Using the instructions that follow make the following diamond units:
(3) light purple with dark purple centers
(4) dark purple with light purple centers
(3) light green with dark green centers
(4) dark green with light green centers
(3) light orange with dark orange centers
(3) dark orange with light orange centers
(3) light red with dark red centers
(3) dark red with light red centers
(3) light blue with dark blue centers
(3) dark blue with light blue centers

Diamond Units

1. Starting with a dark green hexie, add light green and dark green hexies around it to make a standard flower unit as explained on page 18. (See Fig. 1)

2. Join together (3) light green hexies as per Fig. 2. Join this unit to the unit made in step 1. (See Fig. 3)

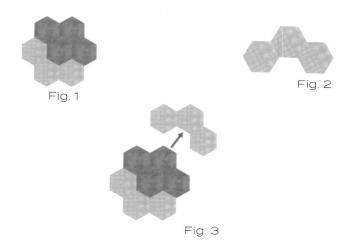

Fig. 1

Fig. 2

Fig. 3

3. Join together (3) light green hexies as per Fig. 4; repeat to make (2) of these units.

4. Join the units made in step 3 to both ends of the unit made in step 2. (See Fig. 5)

5. Repeat steps 1-4 to make the required number of Diamond Units in each of the different colors.

Fig. 4

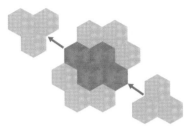

Fig. 5

Partial Diamond Units

1. Starting with a dark blue hexie sew light and dark blue hexies around it to make a standard flower unit. (See Fig. 1)

2. Join together (2) light blue hexies add an additional light blue hexie as per Fig. 2; repeat to make (2) of these units.

3. Join the units made in the previous step to the top and bottom of the standard flower unit. (See Fig. 3)

4. Repeat steps 1-3 substituting dark red were it says dark blue and light red where it says light blue.

Fig. 1

Fig. 2

Fig. 3

Star Units

Following these instructions
make the following units:
(2) Purple Stars
(2) Green Stars
(1) Orange Star
(1) Red Star
(1) Blue Star

 With the new day comes new
strength and new thoughts...
Eleanor Roosevelt

1. Starting with a dark purple hexie, join a row of light purple hexies to it to make a standard flower unit. (See Fig. 1)

2. Join another row to this unit alternating medium and dark purple hexies (See Fig. 2)

3. To the this unit add a row of alternating beige and dark purple hexies. (See Fig. 3)

4. Add a final row to this unit using beige, dark purple, and brown hexies. (See Fig. 4)

5. Join together (1) brown and (1) beige hexie; repeat for a total of 18 units

6. Join together (2) of the units made in step 5; repeat for a total of (6) units. (See Fig. 5)

7. Add an additional brown hexie to the end of a beige/brown hexie unit; repeat for a total of (6) units.(See Fig. 6 page 104)

8. Join together (2) brown hexies; repeat for a total of (6) double brown units.

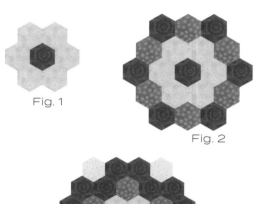

Fig. 1

Fig. 2

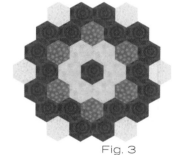

Fig. 3

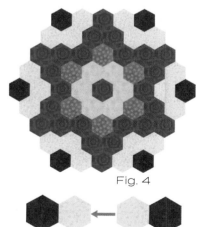

Fig. 4

Fig. 5

9. Using one additional brown hexie, join together the units made in steps 6-8; repeat for a total of (6) units. (See Fig. 7)

10. Sew (1) unit to each side of the standard flower unit made previously. (See Fig. 8)

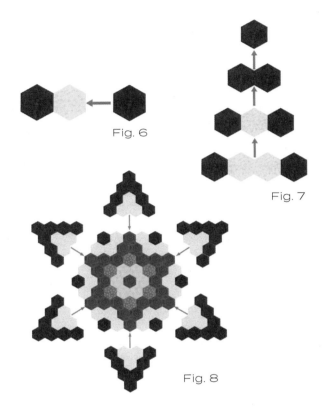

Fig. 6

Fig. 7

Fig. 8

Partial Star Units

Following these instructions make the following units.
(2) blue partial star units
(1) red partial star unit
(1) orange partial star unit.

1. Starting with a dark orange hexie, sew dark orange, medium orange, bright yellow and beige hexies around it to form a standard flower unit. (See Fig. 1)

2. Using brown, beige, dark orange and yellow hexies add another row to this unit. (See Fig. 2)

3. Join together a medium orange hexie and a bright yellow hexie; repeat to make (2) of these double units.

Fig. 1

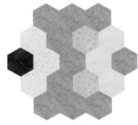

Fig. 2

4. As per Fig. 3, join these units to the unit made in step 2.

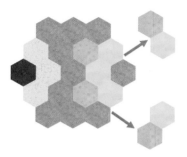

5. Join together (2) beige hexies; repeat to make (2) units.

Fig. 3

6. Join together (2) dark orange units; repeat to make (2) units.

7. Join the units made in steps 5 & 6 together. (See Fig. 4); repeat to make (2) units

Fig. 4

8. Join together (1) beige and (1) brown hexie add a dark orange hexie to the beige hexie. (See Fig. 5)

Fig. 5

9. Join the units made in step 7 & 8 together; repeat to make (2) units. (See Fig. 6)

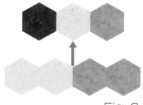

10. Join the units made in step 9 to the unit made in step 4. (See Fig. 7)

Fig. 6

11. Join together (1) beige and (1) brown hexie; repeat to make a total of (9) units.

12. Combine (2) of these units to make a (4) hexie chain; repeat for a total of (2) units. (See Fig. 8)

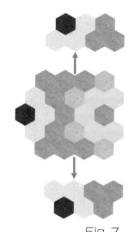

Take a minute to unwind after a long, hard day at work. Better yet; take 5 with the 5 minute unwind on page 148.

Fig. 7

Fig. 8

13. Using (1) of the beige/brown units made in step 11, add an additional brown unit to the end; repeat to make (2) units. (See Fig. 9)

14. Join together (2) brown hexies; repeat for a total of (4) units.

15. Add (1) additional brown unit to the top of the unit made in step 14; repeat for a total of (4) units. (See Fig. 10)

16. Using (1) unit from step 12, 13 & !5, join together as per Fig. 11; repeat for a total of (2) units.

17. Using one of the beige/brown units from step 11, add an additional beige unit to the end; repeat for a total of (2) units. (See Fig. 12)

18. Join the unit made in step 17 to (1) of the remaining beige/brown units; repeat for a total of (2) units. (See Fig. 13)

19. Join this unit to (1) of the units made in step 15; repeat for a total of (2) units (See Fig. 14)

20. Join the units made in step 16 & 19 to the sides of the unit made in step 10) (See Fig 15)

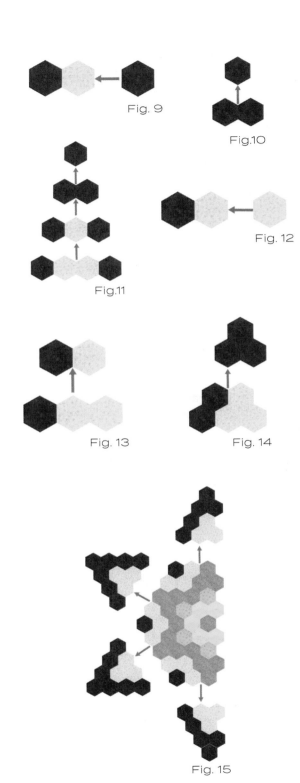

Fig. 9

Fig.10

Fig. 12

Fig.11

Fig. 13

Fig. 14

Fig. 15

Top/bottom Partial Diamond Units

Following these instructions make the following units:

(1) Medium red end cap
(1) Dark blue end cap
(1) Dark green end cap
(1) Dark orange end cap
(1) Dark red end cap
(1) Dark purple end cap

Fig. 1

Fig. 2

1. Join together (2) brown hexies, add an additional brown hexie to the top of this double unit. (See Fig. 1)

2. Join together (1) beige and (1) brown hexie; repeat to make a total of (5) brown/beige double units. Join (1) additional brown hexie to (1) of the double units. (See Fig. 2)

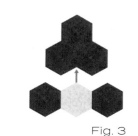

Fig. 3

Fig. 4

3. Join the triple Br/B/Br unit made in step 2 to the unit made in step 1. (See Fig. 3)

4. Join together (2) of the double brown/beige units to form a (4) hexie chain (See Fig. 4)

5. Join this (4) hexie unit to the unit made in step 3. (See Fig. 5)

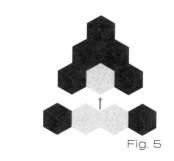

Fig. 5

6. Next join a double beige/brown hexie unit to either side of a dark blue hexie. (See Fig. 6)

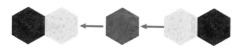

Fig. 6

7. Join the (5) hexie chain made in step 6 to the unit made in step 5. (See Fig. 7)

8. Repeat steps 1-7 substituting the colors listed at the beginning of these instructions for the dark blue hexie.

Fig. 7

Top Assembly

1. Join together (4) brown hexies to form a chain; repeat for a total of (12) brown (4) hexie chains. Add an additional brown hexie to the end of (4) of these chains to make (4) brown (5) hexie chains.

2. Sew one of the (5) hexie chains to the top of a light/dark purple diamond and another to the top of a dark green/light green unit. Join the remaining (2) brown (5) hexie chains to the tops of (2) of the dark purple/ light purple diamonds. (See Fig. 1)

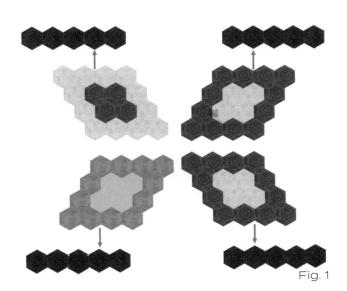

Fig. 1

If you find yourself having a hard time sitting or standing for long periods while working, try the Sphinx pose on page 137. It's great for lower back pain.

3. Join the (4) hexie chains to the top of each of the following units: (See Fig. 2)

   (2) light/dark green diamonds

   (2) light/dark orange diamonds

   (2) dark red/light red diamonds

   (1) dark blue/light blue diamond

   (1) light blue/dark blue diamond

4. Sew together dark/light purple and dark/light green with (5) brown hexies units, red, green and purple top/bottom partial units, and light/dark green, light/dark orange, light/dark blue, and dark red/light red with (4) brown hexies units to make the top row. (See Fig. 3)

Fig. 2

Fig. 3

5. To form the next row, join together (1) partial blue and (1) partial orange star units, (1) dark/light red, (1) dark/light green, and (1) dark/light blue diamonds, with (1) purple star unit and (1) green star unit. (See Fig. 4)

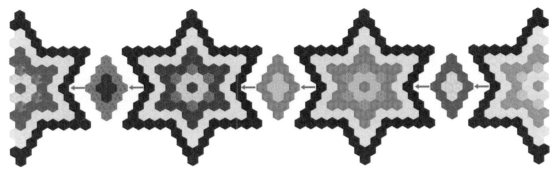

Fig. 4

6. Next, add a brown hexie to the top and bottom of both the red and the blue partial diamond units. (See Fig. 5)

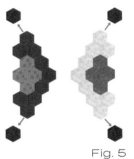

Fig. 5

7. Sew the units made in step 6 to (1) orange star, (1) dark/light purple diamonds, (1) blue star, (1) dark/light green diamonds and (1) red star to make the next row. (See Fig. 6)

Fig. 6

8. To the row made in step 7, join the remaining regular diamond units. (Not the ones with the brown hexies attached.) (See Fig. 7)

Fig. 7

9. To form the next row, sew together (1) red partial star, (1) blue partial star, (1) light/dark purple diamond, (1) green star, (1) light/dark blue diamond, (1) purple star and (1) dark/light orange diamond. (See Fig. 8)

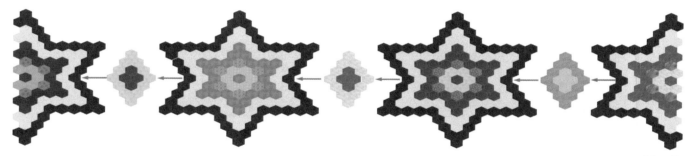

Fig. 8

10. Next, sew together dark/light purple and light/dark purple diamonds with the attached (5) brown hexies, remaining diamonds with the attached (4) brown hexies and the purple, blue, and orange top/bottom partial diamond units. (See Fig. 9)

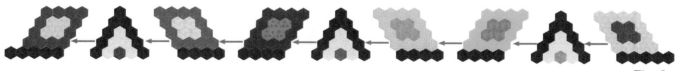

Fig. 9

11. Join the units made in steps 1–10 together to form the quilt top using Fig. 10 and the placement diagram on page 113 as a reference.

Fig. 10

Placement Diagram

Quilting Diagram

Quilt was quilted with loops in the outer border. Continuous curves, loops, and swirls were quilted in the stars and diamonds, and additional filigree designs were added to the diamond centers.

Hexagon Jubilee

Total number of hexagon foundations needed for this project: 1669.

Finished Quilt Size 76" X 85"

Hexie Requirements (1")

- 58 dark purple hexies
- 29 medium purple hexies
- 53 med./dk. purple hexies
- 27 light purple hexies
- 31 dark pink hexies
- 58 red hexies
- 32 medium pink hexies
- 17 light pink hexies
- 63 dark orange hexies
- 31 medium orange hexies
- 27 bright yellow hexies
- 58 med/dark blue hexies
- 29 light/med blue hexies
- 63 dark green hexies
- 32 light/med green hexies
- 29 med/dark green hexies
- 15 light green hexies
- 641 light/med beige hexies
- 376 medium brown hexies

Materials

Yardage is based on 42" wide fabric

- ⅜ yd dark purple print
- ¼ yd med. purple print
- ⅜ yd med/dk. purple print
- ¼ yd lt. purple mottled
- ⅜ yd red print
- ¼ yd dark pink print
- ¼ yd medium pink print
- ¼ yd light pink print
- ⅜ dark orange print
- ¼ yd med. orange print
- ¼ yd bright yellow mottled
- ⅜ yd med/dark blue print
- ¼ yd light/med blue print
- ⅜ yd dark green print
- ¼ yd lt./med green print
- ¼ yd med/dk. green print
- ¼ yd light green print
- 3¾ yds light/med beige
- 2¼ yds medium brown

Assembling the Quilt

A jubilee of hexie flowers that will let you plan a truly colorful garden.

———————✷———————

 Additional fabric: 3 yds coordinating 108 wide fabric for backing and facing strips. After quilting, cut: (4) strips approximately 87" long by 4½" wide from leftover backing fabric

———————✷———————

Prepare the required number of each color hexagons, as per the instructions in the Prepping the Hexies section. (Page 13) If you are facing your quilt instead of binding, do not prep the following number of hexies until the side and top/bottom full/partial flower instructions. (Hexies will need to be cut out using an exact ¼" seam allowance)

(4) dark purple hexies
(5) medium purple hexies
(2) medium/dark purple hexies
(3) light purple hexies
(4) dark red hexies
(6) dark pink hexies
(8) medium pink hexies
(11) light pink hexies
(6) dark orange hexies
(7) medium orange hexies
(4) medium/dark blue hexies
(5) light/medium blue hexies
(6) dark green hexies
(2) medium/dark green hexies
(8) light/medium green hexies
(3) light green hexies
(56) light/medium beige hexies
(22) medium brown hexies

Flower Units

1. Starting with a bright yellow hexie, join light purple hexies around it to form a standard flower unit as per the instructions in Sewing the Hexies page 18. (See Fig. 1)

Fig. 1

2. Next add a row of med/dark purple hexies to the unit made in step 1. (See Fig. 2)

Fig. 2

3. Finish unit by adding a row of light/ med beige hexies. (See Fig. 3)

4. Repeat steps 1-3 to make the following number of standard flower units.

    (4) Dark with Medium Purple Units

    (4) Medium with Light Purple Units

    (4) Dark with Medium Green Units

    (2) Medium with Light Green Units

    (4) Dark with Medium Orange Units

    (4) Dark with Medium Red Units

    (1) Medium with Light Pink Unit

    (4) Dark with Medium Blue Units

Fig. 3

 Take a load off and treat your feet to a home pedicure with this rich tea tree lotion on page 147.

Remaining Units

Before assembling the remaining units, you will need to finish prepping the hexies held in reserve. The hexies will be prepped in one of four ways as per Figs. 1-4. Prep the following hexies for each type.

Type 1 (See Fig. 1)
(4) light/medium green
(2) light green
(2) medium orange
(4) dark pink
(6) light pink
(2) light purple
(2) medium purple
(1) light/medium blue
(20) beige

Type 2 (See Fig. 2)
(1) medium/dark blue
(2) dark blue
(4) dark green
(2) medium/dark green
(1) light green
(6) medium pink
(2) dark pink
(3) light pink
(4) dark red
(2) dark orange
(1) medium orange
(2) dark purple
(2) medium/dark purple
(1) medium purple
(1) light purple
(2) light/medium green
(10) brown

Type 1- Fig. 1

Type 2- Fig. 2

Type 3 (See Fig. 3)
(4) beige

Type 3 -Fig. 3

Type 4: (See Fig. 4)
(2) dark blue
(2) medium blue
(4) dark orange
(4) medium orange
(2) dark green
(2) light/medium green
(2) dark purple
(2) medium purple
(2) light pink
(2) medium pink
(12) brown
(32) beige

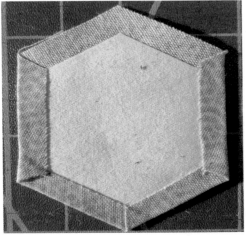

Type 4 – Fig. 4

Stop and take time to breath. Remember this is supposed to be fun and relaxing. Try one of the Yoga pose on page 139 to help relax and reduce stress.

Partial Side Flower Units

For the following instructions, the blue arrow will indicate the sides of the hexies that have not been turned under. (#'s on hexies indicate the type of prep.)

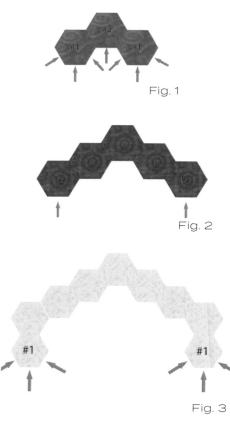

Fig. 1

1. Join together (2) Type 1 and (1) Type 2 medium purple hexies. (See Fig. 1)

Fig. 2

2. Join (2) Type 2 and (3) of the dark purple hexies that were prepped using the standard hexie prep. (See Fig. 2)

3. Sew together (7) standard beige hexies and (2) Type 1 beige hexies. (See Fig. 3)

4. Sew together the units made in step 1–3 as per Fig. 4.

Fig. 3

5. Repeat steps 1–4 to make the following units:

   (2) dark green with light/medium green
   (1) dark with medium purple
   (2) medium pink with light pink
   (1) dark red with dark pink
   (1) dark orange with medium orange
   (1) dark blue with medium blue

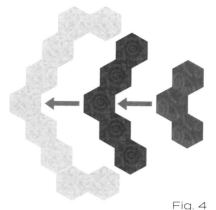

Fig. 4

Top/Bottom Partial Flower Units

For the following instructions, the blue arrow will indicate the sides of the hexies that have not been turned under.

Fig. 1

1. Join together (4) standard prepped beige hexies to make a chain (See Fig. 1)

2. Join together (3) dark orange and (2) beige hexies to make a (5) hexie chain. (See Fig. 2)

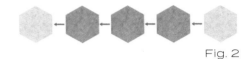
Fig. 2

3. Sew together (2) beige, (2) dark orange, and (2) medium orange Type 4 hexies to form a chain of (6) hexies. (See Fig. 3)

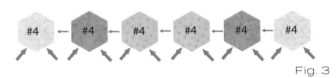
Fig. 3

4. Join the chains made in steps 1-3 together to form the Top/Bottom Unit. (See Fig. 4)

5. Repeat steps 1-4 to make the following units:

   (1) medium pink with light pink
   (1) dark blue with medium blue
   (1) dark purple with medium purple
   (2) dark orange with medium orange
   (1) dark green with light/medium green

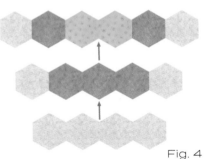
Fig. 4

Don't let people tell you your ideas are stupid. If you're really passionate about something, find a way to build it...
Dennis Crowley

Top/Bottom Flower Units

For the following instructions, the blue arrow will indicate the sides of the hexies that have not been turned under. (#'s on hexies indicate the type of prep.)

Fig. 1

1. Starting with a bright yellow hexie, join light purple hexies around it to form a standard flower unit as per the instructions in Sewing the Hexies page 14. (See Fig. 1)

2. Next add a row of med/dark purple hexies to the unit made in step 1. (See Fig. 2)

Fig. 2

3. Finish unit by adding a row of light/med beige hexies. Note that (4) of these will be the Type 4 prep. (See Fig. 3)

4. Repeat steps 1-3 to make the following Top/ Bottom units;

   (1) additional med/dark purple with
       light purple center
   (1) dark red with dark pink center
   (1) med/dark green with light green center

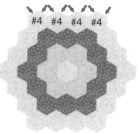

Fig. 3

Corner Flower Units

For the following instructions, the blue arrow will indicate the sides of the hexies that have not been turned under. (#'s on hexies indicate the type of prep.)

Fig. 1

1. Join together (2) Type 1 and (1) Type 2 light green hexies. (See Fig. 1)

2. Join (2) Type 2 and (3) of the med/dark green hexies that were prepped using the standard method. (See Fig. 2)

Fig. 2

3. Sew together (7) standard beige hexies and (1) Type 1, (1) Type 3 and (1) Type 4 beige hexies. (See Fig. 3)

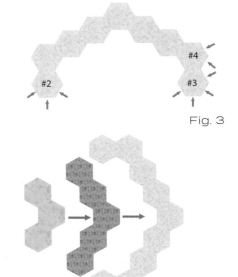
Fig. 3

4. Sew together the units made in step 1-3 as per Fig. 4.

5. Join together (2) Type 1 and (1) Type 2 dark pink hexies. (See Fig. 5)

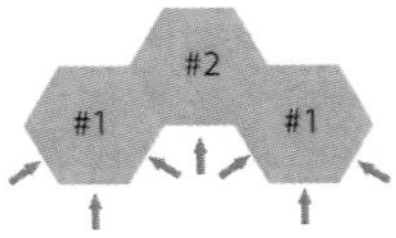

6. Join (2) Type 2 and (3) of the dark red hexies that were prepped using the standard hexie prep. (See Fig. 6)

Fig. 4

7. Sew together (7) standard beige hexies and (1) Type 1, (1) Type 3 and (1) Type 4 beige hexies. (See Fig. 7)

8. Sew together the units made in step 1-3 as per Fig. 8.

Fig. 5

Fig. 6

Fig. 7

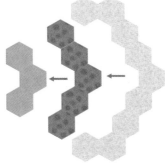

Fig.8

9. Join together (2) Type 1 and (1) Type 2 light pink hexies. (See Fig. 9)

Fig. 9

10. Join (2) Type 2 and (3) of the medium pink hexies that were prepped in the usual way. (See Fig. 10)

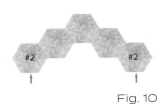
Fig. 10

11. Sew together (7) standard beige hexies and (1) Type 1, (1) Type 3 and (1) Type 4 beige hexies. (See Fig. 11)

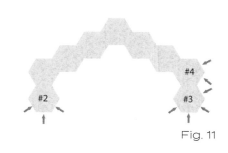

Fig. 11

12. Sew together the units made in step 1-3 as per Fig. 12.

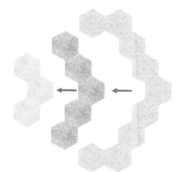

13. Join together (2) Type 1 and (1) Type 2 light purple hexies. (See Fig. 13)

Fig. 12

14. Join (2) Type 2 and (3) of the med/dark purple that were prepped using the standard hexie prep. (See Fig. 14)

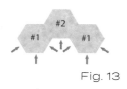

Fig. 13

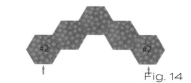

Fig. 14

15. Sew together (7) standard beige hexies and (1) Type 1, (1) Type 3 and (1) Type 4 beige hexies. (See Fig. 15)

16. Sew together the units made in step 1-3 as per Fig. 16.

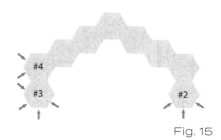

Fig. 15

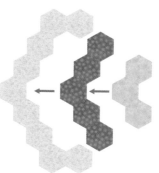

Fig. 16

Assembling the Quilt

1. Join together (3) dark brown hexies to form a chain; repeat for a total of (28) triple brown chains.

2. Join together (4) dark brown hexies to form a chain; repeat for a total of (72) quadruple brown chains.

3. Using the Type 2 brown hexies, join together (2) corner flower units, and (6) of the partial side flower units using Fig. 1 for reference.

Fig. 1

4. To make row 2, join together (2) top/bottom partial flower units (on either end) and (5) flower units, using the dark brown (3) hexie units to connect them. (See Fig. 2)

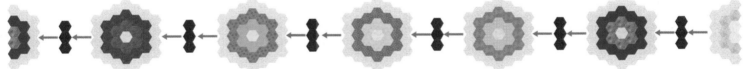

Fig. 2

5. Sew (12) of the dark brown (4) hexie chains to the top of row 2; repeat on the bottom as per Fig. 3.

Fig. 3

6. To form row 3, sew together (4) flower units and (2) top/bottom flower units (on either end), using the dark brown (3) hexie units to connect them. Use Fig. 4 as a reference.

Fig. 4

7. Sew together (5) flower units, and (2) top/bottom partial flower units (on either end) to form row 4, using the dark brown (3) hexie units to connect them (See Fig. 5)

Fig. 5

8. Sew (12) of the dark brown (4) hexie chains to the top of row 4; repeat on the bottom as per Fig. 6.

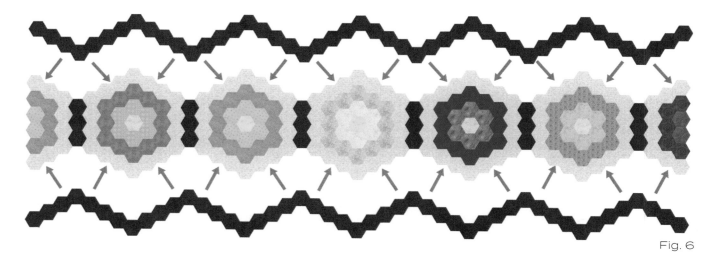

Fig. 6

9. To make row 5, join together (4) flower units and (2) top/bottom flower units (on either end), using the dark brown (3) hexie units to connect them. Use Fig. 7 (Page 128) as a reference.

Fig. 7

10. To make row 6, join together (2) top/bottom partial flower units (on either end) and (5) flower units, using the dark brown (3) hexie units to connect them. (See Fig. 8)

Fig. 8

11. Sew (12) of the dark brown (4) hexie chains to the top of row 2; repeat on the bottom as per Fig. 9.

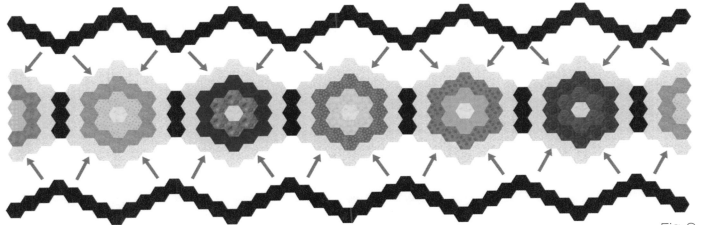

Fig. 9

12. Using the remaining Type 2 brown hexies, join together (2) corner flower units, and (6) of the partial side flower units using Fig. 10.

Fig. 10

13. Sew rows 1–7 together. Using Fig. 11 and placement diagram on page 130 for reference.

Fig. 11

Placement Guideline

Quilting Diagram

Quilt was quilted using continuous curves with a simple swirl into the center of each yellow flower center.

Variation

Yoga Poses

As quilters/sewists we spend lots of time sitting, frequently bent over our machines, or standing at the cutting table. This can cause tension in our back, neck, and shoulders. These poses can help to relieve tension and stress and help smooth the transition between quilting and real life.

Balasana (Child's)

Although it looks easy, Savasana (Corpse Pose) can actually be on of the most difficult yoga poses. You can't just say, "OK, I'm going to relax, right now!" (Just ask anyone who has trouble falling asleep at night.) That's why Savasana is such a gift. This pose sets up the conditions that allow you to gradually enter a truly relaxed state, one that is deeply refreshing in itself and that also can serve as a starting point for meditation.

Contraindications: Back injury

Corpse Pose

In this pose, you will rest your entire body on the floor. Extend your arms and legs outward from the torso evenly and symmetrically. Let your feet relax open and your palms face up. Mentally scan the body from head to toe, gradually releasing each body part and each muscle group; allowing it to relax. Take time to notice all the places where the body is making contact with the floor. With each exhalation, picture each limb getting a little heavier and spreading out a little more. When coming out of this pose, first take a few deep breaths. Give yourself a few moments to regain physical awareness of your arms and legs, and then slowly move your body back to a seated position.

Uttana Shishosana(Extended Puppy Pose)

This pose stretches the spine, shoulders, upper back, and arms, making this pose perfect for those who tend to hold tension in their shoulders and upper back. It is also beneficial for stress and anxiety, as well as chronic tension, and insomnia. As a mild inversion, with the heart slightly higher than the head, this pose can help bring a sense of calm back into the body.

Contraindications: Knee or hip injury

Start on all fours with your shoulders above your wrists and your hips above your knees.

Walk your hands forward. As you exhale, move your buttocks halfway back toward your heels. (Keep your arms active; don't let your elbows touch the ground.)

Extended Puppy Pose

Drop your forehead to the floor and let your neck relax. Keep a slight curve in your lower back. (To feel a nice long stretch in your spine, press the hands down and stretch through the arms while pulling your hips back toward your heels.) Breathe feel your spine lengthen in both directions. Hold for 30 seconds to a minute, then release your buttocks down onto your heels.

If you are very tight in your hips and back, you can modify this pose by not bringing your arms out as far or by keeping your buttocks up higher in the air

Modified extended Puppy Pose

Virabhadrasana II (Warrior II Pose)

This pose is a wonderful stretch for the legs, groin, and chest, It also increases stamina and helps to relieve backaches. This pose strengthens the muscles in the thighs and buttocks, and tones the abdomen, ankles, and arches of the feet. Warrior II also helps to increase your ability to concentrate.

Contraindications: Leg, knee, hip, or shoulder injuries, weak heart, or high blood pressure.

Start from a standing position with your feet together. Take a big step back with your left leg, toes pointing slightly in.

Press the four corners of your feet down, and firm your legs up. As you inhale, raise your arms parallel to the floor, keeping your shoulders down and your neck long.

Warrior 2 Pose

As you exhale, bend your right knee, keeping your knee over your ankle. Draw your stomach in and up and lengthen your spine. Extend through your collarbones and fingertips. Look over your right hand.

Stay in this pose for 5 breaths. To come out of the pose press into your feet and straighten your legs as you inhale. Switch the orientation of your feet and repeat on the other side.

You can modify this pose by not bending your knee as deeply. Work to try and bend your knee more each time you perform this pose.

Modified Warrior 2 Pose

Ardha Pincha Mayurasana (Dolphin)

Dolphin pose strengthens, and stretches the shoulders, upper back and legs. It also helps to strengthen your core. It is a great alternative to Downward Dog if you have wrist issues.

Contraindications: Neck or shoulder injuries; weak back.

Start on all fours. Place your forearms on the floor, your elbows directly under your shoulders. Place the palms of your hands down with your forearms parallel with each other.

As you exhale, curl your toes under. Engage your lower belly and lift your knees away from the floor

Lift your sitting bones up and lengthen the tailbone as you straighten your legs and lower your heels towards the floor.

Engage your thigh muscles and keep your stomach drawn in, press the forearms actively into the floor.

Lengthen your spine. Hold your head between your arms, off the floor. Hold for 10-20 breaths.

To come out of the pose, allow your knees to come back onto the floor as you exhale and rest in Child's Pose.

You can modify the intensity of the stretch in this pose by bending your knees slightly, and not pushing your heels as close to the floor.

Dolphin Pose

Modified Dolphin Pose

Salamba Bhujangasana (Spinx)

This pose strengthens the spine while stretching the front of the chest, the shoulders, and the stomach. It expands the lungs and stimulates the abdominal organs & digestive system and improves blood circulation to rejuvenate your back. Sphinx is a great way to strengthen and tone the glutes.

Contraindications: recent or chronic injury to the back, arms, shoulders or pregnancy. Women who are pregnant may practice the modification.

Lie face down on your stomach and press the tops of your feet firmly down on the mat.

Slide your hands back until your elbows are directly under your shoulders and press up onto your forearms.

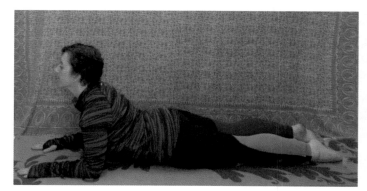

Sphinx Pose

Extend out of the crown of your head and create space between your ears and your shoulders.

Breathe and hold the pose for at least one minute, or longer if it remains comfortable.

You can modify this pose by preforming it in a standing position. Make sure that you keep your stomach tight and don't let your back sway.

Modified Spinx Pose

Salabhasana (Locust)

Locust pose strengthens the legs and core body while opening the chest and stretching the low back. Locust pose purifies the kidneys and stimulates the reproductive and digestive systems.

Contraindications: Injuries to the back, arms or shoulders, pregnancy, or recent abdominal surgery.

Lie on your belly, with your chin on the floor, legs together and arms alongside the body.

Pull up the knee caps, squeeze the thighs and buttocks, and press the pubic bone down into the floor.

Locust Pose

Inhale and lift the legs, head, chest, and arms off of the floor. Reach out through the fingers, toes and crown of the head. Keep the neck in line with the spine.

Drop the shoulders down and back and press the chest forward.

Breathe and hold for 2-6 breaths.

Exhale and slowly lower the chest, head, arms and legs to the floor.

This pose can be modified by not lifting your legs and head/shoulders as high and placing a rolled towel under your chest.

Modified Locust Pose

Adho Mukha Svanasana (Down Dog)

This pose stretches the hamstrings and calves. It strengthens the arms, legs, and back. It can help relieve back pain. The pose also strengthens the deep abdominal muscles that help stabilize the spine.

Contraindications: Heart disease, slipped disc, or other spinal injury:

Come to your hands and knees with the wrists underneath the shoulders and the knees underneath the hips.

Curl your toes under and push back through your hands to lift your hips and straighten your legs. Spread your fingers to help with your balance.

Engage your quadriceps strongly to take the burden of your body's weight off your arms.

Don't worry if you can't get your heels all the way to the floor.

Hold for 10-20 breaths. Exhale and bend your knees to release and come back to your hands and knees.

Modify this pose by keeping your knees slightly bent and your heels off the floor.

Down Dog Pose

Modified Down Dog

Utthita Trikonasana(Extended Triangle)

This pose stretches the legs, groin, hips, shoulders, chest and spine, and strengthens the feet, ankles and legs. Regular practice of this pose may help to alleviate stress and anxiety.

Contraindications: Back, neck or hamstring injury; low or high blood pressure

Begin standing at the top of your mat with your feet together and hands at side.

Exhale, step your left foot back about 3 to 4 feet, placing it parallel to the back edge of your mat.

Angle your left foot in slightly and line up the heel of your right foot with the heel of your left foot. With straight legs, tighten your thighs without locking your knees.

Extended Triangle Pose

Inhale, bend at the hip, bring your right hand down. Reach your left arm straight up toward the ceiling. Root down evenly through the floor

Keep your head in a neutral position or look up toward your left hand if it feels comfortable for your neck.

Remain in the pose for 5 full breaths. Inhale, look down and return to a standing position. Step forward to the top of your mat. Reverse your feet and repeat on the opposite side.

You can modify this pose by using a yoga block and not spreading your feet as widely.

Modified Extended Triangle Pose

Just Breathe

In today's crazy world it's more important than ever to make sure that you take time to stop and "Just Breathe". Setting aside a time to rest and recharge will help to make everything seem more manageable. Here are some simple recipes to help you decrease stress and rejuvenate.

Lavender and Olive Oil Soap

Homemade soap is a wonderful way to treat your skin to a rejuvenating pick me up without all those harsh chemicals that dry you out.

The Recipe-

Use a good quality pure olive oil soap as the base. Enrich with oil and scent with lavender to create a rejuvenating cleanser.

    6 oz. olive oil soap
    1 1/2 tsp. coconut oil
    1 1/2 tsp. almond oil
    2 tbsp. ground almonds
    10 drops lavender essential oil

Grate the soap and place in a double boiler. Soften soap over a low heat. When soft, add remaining ingredients and mix well. Press the mixture into oiled molds and leave to set over night. Remove from mold when set.

 Tip: Always check for allergic reactions before using a new lotion or beauty product.

Citrus Body Scrub

This invigorating body scrub made with orange peal and sea salt is the perfect blend to make you feel refreshed and ready to go. This reviving scrub helps to remove dead skin cells and stimulate the blood supply to the skin.

The Recipe-
3 tbsp freshly ground sunflower seeds
3 tbsp medium oatmeal
3 tbsp. flaked sea salt
3 tbsp finely grated orange peel
3 drops grapefruit essential oil
almond oil

Mix together all the ingredients except the almond oil and store in a sealed glass jar. When ready to use, mix a small amount at a time with some almond oil to make a thick paste and rub over damp skin. Rinse and pat dry with a towel.

Luscious Rose Night Cream

This luscious night cream helps to replenish and revive dry skin. Jasmine and rose oils help to rehydrate skin, while frankincense helps to reduce wrinkles and improve tone.

The Recipe-
20 ox jar of unperfumed base cream with a tight fitting lid
3 drops rose essential oil
2 drops frankincense essential oil
1 drop jasmine essential oil

Add oils to cream and mix until well blended. Apply a small amount of cream to face right before bed, and gently rub in using light feathery strokes.

Coconut and Orange Flower Lotion

This lush and creamy body lotion is great for soothing and nourishing dry skin. The wheatgerm oil is rich in Vitamin E, and antioxidant that protects against premature aging.

The Recipe-
2 oz coconut oil
4 tbsp sunflower oil
2 tsp wheatgerm oil
10 drops orange essential oil.

Melt the coconut oil in a heatproof bowl over gently simmering water. Stir in sunflower and wheatgerm oil. Allow to cool. When coo, add orange essential oil and pour into seal-able glass jar. The lotion will solidify over several hours.

Tip: Label and date home-made lotions. It is generally good for a month if stored in a sealed bottle in a cool place, but it will not keep indefinitely.

Rose Facial Scrub

This luxurious blend of almonds, oatmeal, and rose petals gently cleanses your face while leaving it feeling silky soft.

If you are using rose petals from your own garden make sure that they have not been sprayed with any pesticides.

The Recipe-

Makes enough for 8-10 uses
3 tbsp ground almonds (Without skin)
3 tbsp medium oatmeal
3 tbsp powdered milk
2 tbsp powdered rose petals
almond oil

Mix all ingredients except almond oil in a bowl until thoroughly combined. Store mixture in a sealed glass jar until ready to use.

To use: mix a small handful of the mixture and blend together with a little almond oil until a soft paste is formed. Gently rub the scrub into damp skin, using a circular motion and avoiding the skin around your eyes. Rinse facial scrub thoroughly and then gently pat face dry with a soft towel.

Tip: Always check for allergic reactions before using a new lotion or beauty product.

Relaxing Herbal Bath

This gentle and relaxing herbal bath helps to purify and gently cleanse your skin.

The herbs can be bought from the store on grown in your own herb garden or window box. Use fresh herbs whenever possible.

The Recipe-
7 basil leaves
3 bay leaves
3 sprigs oregano
1 sprig tarragon
2 tsp organic oats
pinch rock or sea salt
small square cotton muslin
thread to tie up muslin

Pile the herbs in the center of the muslin square and sprinkle with the oats. Top with the rock or sea salt. Pick up corners of muslin and tie with thread. Hang the sachet from the bath tap so that the water will run over the bag an infuse the tub with the essence of the mixture.

Tea Tree Foot Cream

Relax and take a load off while you pamper your feet with this rich foot cream. Tea tree essential oil is a must for foot creams with its healing antiseptic properties and effective fungicidal action.

The Recipe-
    4 oz. unscented cream
    15 drops tea tree essential oil

Blend the essential oil thoroughly into the unscented cream and add to a plastic bottle with a pump. Make sure to label and date the bottle. Rub cream into each foot as needed.

Quick De-stress

It's easy to come home from work and let yourself be drawn directly into the fray- cooking, cleaning, laundry, homework help etc. The last thing you're probably thinking about is how to unwind, but this simple 5 minute routine, will help you to relax and focus on the moment so that you can enjoy your time at home instead of feeling overwhelmed by it.

Step 1

1. Stretching your neck–
    Cradle your neck in a warmed, rolled towel. Arch your head back and hold for 2-3 breaths.

2. Stretching your neck and shoulders–
    Pull the ends of the towel down and wrap it around your shoulders. Press your fists into the small of your back, pulling your elbows together to increase the pressure and expand the chest. Hole for 2-3 breaths. (Repeat steps 1 & 2 six times)

Step 2

3. Pressing your body–
    Sitting on the floor, hold the rolled towel down your spine. Tuck one end under your buttocks and hold the other end extended over your head. Slowly ease your body down on to the floor on top of the towel, centering your spine over the end. Release the top end of the towel, bend your knees and place your hands on your hips. Rest and relax allowing the muscles on either side of the rolled towel to open and relax with the pull of gravity. Stay in this position for 2-3 minutes

Step 3

4. Release the pressure–
    Put two tennis balls into a sock and knot the top. Press the balls into the tight muscles on either side of your spine at the base of your back and hold for 2-3 breaths.

Step 4

Resources

The tools and supplies shown in this book are from the following manufactures and can be found at your local fabric or craft store, Wal-mart, or on the Web.

Quilter On the Run
3807 NW 63rd Terrace
Kansas City, MO 64151
402-613-8545
www.quilterontherun.com

Superior Threads
87 East 2580 South
St. George, Utah 84790
435-652-1867 or 800-499-1777
www.superiorthreads.com

Nancy's Notions
333 Beichl Ave.
P.O. Box 683
Beaver Dam, WI 53916-0683
800.833.0690
www.nancysnotions.com

Elmer's™ School Glue
4110 Premier Drive
High Point, NC 27265
1-888-435-6377
www.elmers.com

Brother™ Scan and Cut
877-276-8437
www.brother-usa.com

AccuCut™
8843 S. 137th Circle
Omaha, NE 68138
800-288-1670
www.accucut.com

Reynolds Freezer Paper™
http://www.reynoldskitchens.com/freezer-paper/

About the Author

Kris Vierra has been a quilter/seamstress for over 20 years, and a professional longarm quilter for more than a decade. She teaches at national shows and guilds across the country, and has won numerous national/international awards for her machine quilting skills over the years.

Most recently, Kris was awarded Best Longarm Quilting at AQS Paducah 2018, AQS Phoenix 2016, and AQS Des Moines 2016, and the PFAFF Master Award for Machine Artistry at the Houston International Quilt Festival in 2015.

Kris' classes focus on teaching quilter's how to expand their knowledge base and break out of their comfort zone. She teaches a variety of quilting classes from appliqué/piecing classes, to starting and growing your own longarm business using social media, and everything in between. She believes quilting should be fun and not stressful.

In addition to her love of everything quilting, she is also an avid Yoga practitioner and studied Yoga at the Bhakti Yogshala School of Yoga.

Acknowledgments

I would like to thank my family for their support and patience. My children, who helped out around the house so I could write, and my husband whose encouragement and faith in me helped me to make it through this process. Special thanks go out to my friends Cheri and Debbie. Their input and knowledge of quilting and design was invaluable.

Made in the USA
Columbia, SC
22 February 2021